Scribes and Scripture

J. Harold Greenlee

Scribes and Scripture

New Testament Essays in Honor of J. Harold Greenlee

Edited by
David Alan Black

Eisenbrauns
Winona Lake, Indiana
1992

Library of Congress Cataloging-in-Publication Data

Scribes and scripture : New Testament essays in honor of
J. Harold Greenlee / edited by David Alan Black.
    p.   cm.
Includes bibliographical references and index.
ISBN 0-931464-70-6
    1. Bible.   N.T.—Criticism, interpretation, etc.   I. Greenlee,
J. Harold (Jacob Harold), 1918–   .   II. Black, David Alan,
1952–   .
BS2395.S34   1992   92-2921
225.4—dc20

CONTENTS

Preface

This volume owes its existence to the desire of friends and colleagues of J. Harold Greenlee to express to him the affection and esteem in which he is held as a Christian gentleman and scholar. While only a small portion of Dr. Greenlee's scholarly friends and colleagues is represented here, the range of topics in this volume reflect the diversity of the honoree's talents in the fields of New Testament textual criticism, Greek exegesis, and Bible translation. The quality of the essays and the contributors' ready enthusiasm to join the editor in producing this Festschrift are testimony to the high regard in which Dr. Greenlee is held by all the scholarly community. Many others, including former colleagues and current associates, have expressed their desire to extend to Dr. Greenlee and his wife Ruth their greetings and warm wishes on the occasion of the publication of this volume.

This Festschrift is addressed to all those persons interested in what Dr. Greenlee has exemplified so well through forty-five years of teaching and writing: *vivere et studere ad maiorem Dei gloriam*. It would be difficult to imagine one in whom the erudition of the university and the gentleness of the Spirit more closely cohere than in the life and ministry of this true doctor of the church. As a writer he is perhaps best known for his *Introduction to New Testament Textual Criticism* and his *Concise Exegetical Grammar of New Testament Greek*, books that have endeared him to many a Greek student through the years. His more technical writings, especially those published in the distinguished series Studies and Documents (*The Gospel Text of Cyril of Jerusalem* and *Nine Uncial Palimpsests of the Greek New Testament*), have made a major contribution to the science of New Testament textual

criticism. In addition, he has been a willing and able consultant to
Wycliffe Bible Translators, demonstrating in such unlikely places as
the jungles of Papua New Guinea the true meaning of theological
wisdom. Throughout his ministry as scholar and missionary he has
sought to serve a church that is called to reach a lost world redemp-
tively with the Good News of Jesus Christ.

   It is the pleasant duty of the editor to express his gratitude to a
number of persons, first and foremost to all the contributors to this
volume. The expert typesetting of Eisenbrauns is well known to
scholars of many lands, and warm gratitude is expressed to Jim
Eisenbraun and his competent staff for the opportunity to publish
this Festschrift. Finally, heartfelt thanks are tendered to the honoree
himself for supplying the editor with his curriculum vitae on very
short notice.

David Alan Black

J. Harold Greenlee: Curriculum Vitae and Bibliography

J. Harold Greenlee was born on May 12, 1918, in Charleston, West Virginia, the first of three children of godly parents Jacob A. and Ethel Edith (Jarrett) Greenlee. From the age of six weeks his parents took him to Sunday School and church services at Central Methodist Church, which began a lifelong habit for him. At the age of ten he received Jesus Christ as his Savior in a revival meeting at his church.

In 1949 he married Ruth Bernice Olney, a Methodist minister's daughter, who had been a school teacher, a Navy WAVE officer, and was a graduate in nursing. Their children are Dorothy (Mrs. William Morrison), Lois (Mrs. James Stuck), and David (married to Verena Schranz).

After graduating from Charleston High School he enrolled in Asbury College, where he majored in chemistry. Afterward he enrolled in Asbury Theological Seminary, although he had heard no audible "call to preach." From almost his first day in Greek class he felt that the Lord was leading him to teach Greek—and New Testament Greek has been his principal field of work ever since, having served as professor of Greek in Asbury Theological Seminary for over twenty years. He was ordained a Methodist minister in the West Virginia Conference in 1944, but he has always served in "special appointments" rather than as a pastor.

On two occasions he accepted invitations to teach for brief periods in the OMS seminary in Medillin, Colombia. In this way he was led to become a full-time missionary with OMS in 1969, with the

Greek New Testament as his principal ministry until the present time. OMS has permitted him to serve also as a translation consultant with Wycliffe Bible Translators and the Summer Institute of Linguistics. For the past twenty years he has taught in OMS seminaries and other theological schools in various OMS fields, including Brazil, Ecuador, Japan, Korea, the Philippines, Indonesia, Hong Kong, India, Greece, France, and Spain. He has also served as a translation consultant for WBT/SIL in England, Canada, Mexico, Guatemala, Colombia, Peru, Brazil, the Philippines, Papua New Guinea, Australia, Thailand, Burma, Cameroon, and the Ivory Coast. He continues to serve in the preparation of helps for Bible translators at the International Linguistics Center in Dallas.

Education and Honors

A.B., Asbury College, 1939
B.D., Asbury Theological Seminary, 1943
M.A., University of Kentucky, 1944
Ph.D., Harvard University, 1947
Senior Fulbright Fellow, Oxford University, 1950–51
Summer Institute of Linguistics, University of Oklahoma, 1960
Recipient of Distinguished Alumnus Award, Asbury Theological Seminary, 1956
Recipient of Alumni "A" Award, Asbury College, 1979

Ministry

Professor of New Testament Greek, Asbury Theological Seminary, 1944–65
Professor of New Testament Greek, Oral Roberts University Graduate School of Theology, 1965–69
Professor, Biblical Seminary of Colombia, 1963, 1965, 1969–74
Research Associate, United Bible Societies, 1955–66
Visiting Professor, Winona Lake School of Theology, 1962, 1964
Adjunct Professor of Linguistics, University of Texas at Arlington, 1976–present
Missionary, Oriental Missionary Society (now OMS International), 1969–present
International Translation Consultant, Wycliffe Bible Translators and the Summer Institute of Linguistics, 1971–present
Ordained Minister, United Methodist Church, West Virginia Conference, 1944–present

Publications

Books

The Gospel Text of Cyril of Jerusalem. Studies and Documents 17. Copenhagen: Munksgaard, 1955.

Here and There in the Greek New Testament. London: United Bible Societies, 1956.

A Concise Exegetical Grammar of New Testament Greek. Grand Rapids: Eerdmans, 1963.

An Introduction to New Testament Textual Criticism. Grand Rapids: Eerdmans, 1964.

Nine Uncial Palimpsests of the Greek New Testament. Studies and Documents 39. Salt Lake City: University of Utah Press, 1968.

Secretos Claves de Términos Bíblicos. Translated by H. O. Espinoza. Kansas City: Nazarene Publishing House, 1969.

A New Testament Greek Morpheme Lexicon. Grand Rapids: Zondervan, 1983.

Scribes, Scrolls, and Scripture. Grand Rapids: Eerdmans, 1985.

An Exegetical Summary of Titus and Philemon. Dallas: Summer Institute of Linguistics, 1989.

An Exegetical Summary of Philippians. Dallas: Summer Institute of Linguistics, 1992

Book Adaptations

Spanish adaptation (with H. Burden) of *New Testament Greek for Beginners,* by J. Gresham Machen. Medellin, Colombia: privately printed, 1971.

Spanish adaptation (with H. Burden) of *A Concise Exegetical Grammar of New Testament Greek.* Medellin, Colombia: privately printed, 1971.

Major Articles

""Ἵνα Substantive Clauses in the New Testament," *Asbury Seminarian* 2 (1947) 154–63.

"The Background of the Greek New Testament," *Asbury Seminarian* 3 (1948) 73–77.

"Sin and Sinfulness: A Study in New Testament Terminology," *Asbury Seminarian* 4 (1949) 109–13 [with G. A. Turner].

"The Genitive Case in the New Testament," *Bible Translator* 1 (1950) 68–70.

"The Greek Definite Article," *Asbury Seminarian* 5 (1950) 59–60.

"Κύριος, 'Lord,'" *Bible Translator* 1 (1950) 106–8.

"'Christian Communism' in the Book of Acts," *Asbury Seminarian* 5 (1950) 92–94.

"The Genitive Case in the New Testament," *Asbury Seminarian* 5 (1950) 108–9.

"The Greek Definite Article," *Bible Translator* 1 (1950) 162–65.

"Ψυχή in the New Testament," *Bible Translator* 2 (1951) 73–75.

"Word Suffixes in the Greek New Testament," *Bible Translator* 2 (1951) 159–61.

"The Preposition εἰς in the New Testament," *Bible Translator* 3 (1952) 12–14.

"Verbs in the New Testament," *Bible Translator* 3 (1952) 71–75.

"Christian *Life* Answers *Look* Magazine," *Christian Life* 14 (1952) 30.

"Evangelicals and 'The New Version,'" *United Evangelical Action* 11 (1952) 5–6, 8.

"The Revised Standard New Testament," *Asbury Seminarian* 7 (1953) 29–45.

"New Testament Participles," *Bible Translator* 5 (1954) 98–101.

"My Father," *The Christian Minister* 6 (1954) 25–27.

"'Ίνα Clauses and Related Expressions," *Bible Translator* 6 (1955) 12–16.

"My Father," *Bible Translator* 6 (1955) 119–21.

"I Am," *The Christian Minister* 6 (1955) 13–15.

"What Does the Word 'Holy' Mean?" *The Christian Minister* 7 (1955) 4–8.

"'Christian Communism' in the Book of Acts," *The Christian Minister* 7 (1955) 14–16.

"Two New Testament References to the Eternity of Jesus," *The Christian Minister* 7 (1955) 17–19.

"A Corrected Collation of Codex Zacynthius (Cod. Ξ)," *Journal of Biblical Literature* 76 (1957) 237–41.

"A Misinterpreted *Nomen Sacrum* in P⁹," *Harvard Theological Review* 51 (1958) 187.

"Some Examples of Scholarly 'Agreement in Error,'" *Journal of Biblical Literature* 77 (1958) 363–64.

"Christian Communism in the Book of Acts," in *The Evangelical Commentary: Acts*, by C. W. Carter and R. Earle (Grand Rapids: Zondervan, 1959) 66–68.

"The Catena of Codex Zacynthius," *Biblica* 40 (1959) 992–1001.

"Εἰς μνημόσυνον αὐτῆς, 'for her memorial': Matt. 26:13, Mark 14:9," *Expository Times* 71 (1960) 245.

"If," *Bible Translator* 13 (1962) 39–43.

"Greek Conditional Sentences," *Bible Translator* 13 (1962) 223–24.

"The Greek New Testament and the Message of Holiness," in *Further Insights into Holiness*, edited by K. Geiger (Kansas City: Beacon Hill, 1963) 73–87.

"Texts and Versions (New Testament)," in *The Pictorial Bible Dictionary*, edited by M. C. Tenney (Grand Rapids: Zondervan, 1963) 842–45.

"The Virgin Birth," in *The Validity of the Virgin Birth*, by H. A. Hanke (Grand Rapids: Zondervan, 1963) 109–10.

"The Greek New Testament in Preaching," *Asbury Seminarian* 16 (1963) 17–27.

"Gospel of the Third Dimension," *His* 24 (1964) 1–3, 11.

"No, You Don't Have to Know Greek," *His* 25 (1965) 34–35.

"Erased Greek Manuscripts," *Oral Roberts University Outreach* 3 (1966) 22–23.

"My Call to the Ministry," in *My Call to the Ministry*, edited by C. A. Joyce (London: Marshall, Morgan, and Scott, 1968) 69–74.

"The Importance of Syntax for the Proper Understanding of the Sacred Text of the New Testament," *Evangelical Quarterly* 44 (1972) 131–46.

"A Missionary Named Yaesu," *OMS Outreach* (April 1973) 13–14.

"Some 'Workshop Notes' on Ephesians," *Notes on Translation* 55 (1975) 13–21.

"Codex 0269, a Palimpsest Fragment of Mark," in *Studies in New Testament Language and Text*, edited by J. K. Elliott (Leiden: Brill, 1976) 235–38.

"II Corinthians (the Editorial 'We')," *Notes on Translation* 60 (1976) 31–32.

"The Language of the New Testament," in *The Expositor's Bible Commentary*, edited by F. E. Gaebelein (Grand Rapids: Zondervan, 1979) 1:409–16.

"The New Testament and Homosexuality," in *What You Should Know about Homosexuality*, edited by C. W. Keysor (Grand Rapids: Zondervan, 1979) 79–114.

"First Corinthians: Some Random Notes from Translation Workshop, Ukarumpa [Papua New Guinea], 1978," *Notes on Translation* 82 (1981) 19–29.

"A Note on 'Knowledge'," *Selected Technical Articles Related to Translation* 6 (1982) 30–31.

"A Further Note on Matthew 1:19," *Notes on Translation* 107 (1985) 23–25.

"Purpose and Result," *Notes on Translation* 107 (1985) 25–29.

"Onesiphorus—Friend or Failure?" *Notes on Translation* 108 (1985) 6–9.

"If," *Notes on Translation* 108 (1985) 10–15.

"The End of the Quotation in John 3," *Notes on Translation* 108 (1985) 15–16.

"Husband of One Wife," *Notes on Translation* 108 (1985) 17–18.

"Texts and Manuscripts of the New Testament," in *International Standard Bible Encyclopedia*, edited by G. W. Bromiley (Grand Rapids: Zondervan, 1988) 4:814–22.

"What the New Testament Says About Homosexuality," *Answers to Your Questions about Homosexuality*, edited by C. Lanning (Wilmore: Bristol, 1988) 53–75.

Book Reviews

The Practical Use of the Greek New Testament (K. S. Wuest), *Asbury Seminarian* 2 (1947) 187.

Revision or New Translation? (O. T. Allis), *Asbury Seminarian* 3 (1948) 160–61.

Women in the Old Testament (N. Lofts), *Asbury Seminarian* 5 (1950) 36–37.

The Gospels: An Expanded Translation (K. S. Wuest), *Bible Translator* 9 (1958) 42–44.

Flatland (E. A. Abbott), *Asbury Seminarian* 12 (1958) 42–43.

Communism: Its Faith and Fallacies (J. D. Bales), *Asbury Seminarian* 17 (1963) 98.

The New Testament in Plain English (C. K. Williams), *Recent Books* 6 (1964) n.p.

The New Testament in the Language of Today (W. F. Beck), *Recent Books* 6 (1964) n.p.

The New American Standard Bible: New Testament, Recent Books 6 (1964) n.p.

The Text of the New Testament: Its Transmission, Corruption, and Restoration (B. M. Metzger), *Reformed Journal* (July–August 1964) 24.

Biblical Greek: Illustrated by Examples (M. Zerwick), *Journal of Biblical Literature* 83 (1964) 332–33.

Chapters in the History of New Testament Textual Criticism (B. M. Metzger), *Asbury Seminarian* 19 (1965) 62.

Theological Dictionary of the New Testament, volume 1 (edited by G. Kittel, translated by G. W. Bromiley), *Asbury Seminarian* 19 (1965) 67–68.

I Believe in Miracles (K. Kullman), *Asbury Seminarian* 19 (1965) 68.

Today's English Version of the New Testament (R. G. Bratcher) and *The Oxford Annotated Bible with the Apocrypha: Revised Standard Version* (edited by H. G. May and B. M. Metzger), *Christianity Today* (December 23, 1966) 29–30 (317–18).

Which Bible? (edited by D. O. Fuller), *Notes on Translation* 47 (1973) 15–16.

Marriage and Divorce: What the Bible Says (J. M. Efird), *Good News* (May–June 1985) 54.

Dictionary of Latin and Greek Theological Terms (R. A. Muller), *Notes on Translation* 110 (1985) 33–34.

Manners and Customs of the Bible (J. M. Freeman), *Notes on Translation* 111 (1986) 26.

Greek-English Lexicon of the New Testament Based on Semantic Domains (edited by J. P. Louw and E. A. Nida), *Notes on Translation* 3 (1989) 55–59.

Additional Contributions

Abridgement of "Bethany beyond Jordan (John 1:28)" (P. Parker), *Bible Translator* 9 (1958) 137–38.

Abridgement of "God's Only Son: The Translation of John 3:16 in the RSV" (D. Moody), *Bible Translator* 10 (1959) 1–3.

Bibliography of New Testament Greek, *Asbury Seminarian* 17 (1963) 21–25.

Contributions to *The Greek New Testament* (United Bible Societies): assembling textual variants materials, revision of minor punctuation, assistance in punctuation apparatus and Bible cross-references, and proofreading of text and apparatus.

Numerous brief articles in *Good News, The Herald, Our Faith Today, Wycliffe Bible Encyclopedia,* and *Zondervan's New Compact Bible Dictionary.*

Textual-Exegetical Observations on 1 Corinthians 1:2, 2:1, and 2:10

Gordon D. Fee

Regent College

I take this opportunity to honor Dr. Greenlee by elaborating on three textual questions in 1 Corinthians, beyond what I was able merely to outline in my commentary (Fee 1987). In each case the textual issue has bearing on the exegesis of the passage in particular—and therefore on its proper translation—as well as on some larger questions of meaning in 1 Corinthians as a whole.[1] In pursuing such questions I hope to illustrate by example a major concern of Dr. Greenlee's: that textual criticism is not an end in itself, but must ultimately be brought to bear on the meaning and message of the NT.

1 Corinthians 1:2

The textual variant in question is a matter of word order. Did Paul write "to the church of God which is in Corinth, sanctified in Christ

---

1. The variants have further in common that they are three of nineteen instances where I have opted for a text different from that found in the modern "standard text" (UBS[3]–NA[26]). They also represent the (only) two instances where I differ with both UBS[3]–NA[26] and Zuntz 1953.

1

Gordon D. Fee

Jesus" (variant 1; supported by $\mathfrak{P}^{61}$ ℵ A D Maj lat sy$^{(P)}$ co), or "to the church of God, sanctified in Christ Jesus, which is in Corinth" (variant 2; supported by $\mathfrak{P}^{46}$ B D* F G b m Ambrosiaster)? In relating the divided opinion of the UBS committee, Metzger (1971: 543) says that variant 2,

> though supported by a notable combination of witnesses . . . , appeared to the majority of the Committee to be intrinsically too difficult, as well as quite un-Pauline in comparison with the style of the salutations in other Pauline letters. The reading apparently arose through the accidental omission of one or more phrases and their subsequent reintroduction at the wrong position.

On this point the majority of the committee were influenced by Zuntz (1953: 91–92), who had previously argued:

> This is really more than a mere variation of order. As arranged in $\mathfrak{P}^{46}$ &c., the clauses make a jumble which defies interpretation. This jumble cannot have come about, at this place, by mere scribal slips in these outstanding witnesses. . . . Variants of this kind arise through the insertion of additional or the reintroduction of omitted words. At some very early stage, or even originally, one of the two clauses must have been absent from the text. . . . [The] impossible reading [of $\mathfrak{P}^{46}$] is most easily accounted for if the "sanctified"-clause is supposed to have been absent from some ancestor manuscript; it could penetrate into the text at this unsuitable point if in some less distant ancestor it had been added above the text or in the margin.

Zuntz goes on to argue that the "sanctified" clause is probably not original with Paul, since "οἱ ἡγιασμένοι is not a Pauline term to describe believers."

Three observations, however, are in order:

1. The external evidence strongly favors variant 2, which is also, as Zuntz himself recognized, decidedly the lectio difficilior. Indeed, this combination of earliest and best manuscripts both east and west supporting the harder reading would ordinarily be decisive. Again, as Zuntz has rightly seen, the combination of $\mathfrak{P}^{46}$ and the western evidence puts this reading back very early and must be accounted for. On the other side, the evidence for variant 1 is basically Egyptian and Byzantine.[2] In any case, it is

2. It is doubtful whether the "lat" of NA[26] is a useful siglum, since it represents the Vulgate and two Old Latin manuscripts (a [9th cent.] and r [6th/7th cent.]). This may reflect later influences or may be of little value at all, since it could easily be a "translational" variant, such as one would tend to find in any modern English translation of variant 1.

arguable that one would need considerable and good reasons to overturn the ordinary canons of NT textual criticism for this variant. The question is whether the proffered arguments are that weighty.

2. The primary reason for rejecting the lectio difficilior comes under the rubric of intrinsic probability—it seems too difficult. By this is meant that one can scarcely imagine Paul to have written variant 2. To this Zuntz adds the alleged evidence of Paul's not referring to believers as "the sanctified," thus casting suspicion on the phrase altogether.

3. Zuntz has the integrity to admit that variant 2 is equally difficult to account for under the ordinary canons of transcriptional probability. No scribe would intentionally have created variant 2 from variant 1. Therefore, it must have been accidental, but not by any one of the scribes responsible for our present witnesses, since any mere scribal slip "in these outstanding witnesses . . . would have been quickly mended" (Zuntz 1953: 91). Thus Zuntz resorts to a three- or four-stage process:

a. Either variant 1 or the next stage (b) is original.

b. Very early on one or the other of the phrases, or both, was dropped accidentally.

c. Another scribe, having the text of step *b* in hand, but also aware of the text of step *a*, reinserted the missing clause, but carelessly put it in the wrong place.

d. The text of step *c* had a very early and very wide circulation but was finally overcome by the original itself.

But there are considerable difficulties with this view of things. First, as to transcriptional probabilities: It is nearly impossible to account for any direct corruption moving in the direction of variant 1 to variant 2. That is, variant 2 simply cannot be explained on the basis of variant 1 alone. On the other hand, the opposite is perfectly explicable. Any number of scribes could have—indeed would have—"corrected" variant 2 if it had been original. It is inevitable that variant 1 should finally triumph.

Therefore, in order to get from variant 1 to variant 2, Zuntz must theorize the unlikely possibility of a double error of rare kinds,[3] and then argue that the text based on the double error had such widespread early circulation that it took years for the original to overtake it—although it had to have existed side by side—and

---

3. That is, omission of a considerable piece of text, followed by its reintroduction at the wrong place. On the one hand, there is no easy way to account for either phrase's having been dropped out accidentally; and why would anyone have done so on purpose? On the other hand, reintroduction from an interlinear correction or marginal note is explicable; but in its position in variant 2? Why should something "impossible" for Paul be somehow easier for a scribe—especially since Paul arguably would have been dictating, and thus open to such disjunction, whereas a scribe might be expected to show more care?

that the intermediate stage (the text with the omission, which makes perfectly good sense) had no further known existence. No wonder Zuntz himself ultimately preferred the intermediate-stage text as the Pauline original.

Finally, since someone had to create the text of variant 2, either Paul or a subsequent scribe, why is it inherently more probable for a scribe to have done it than Paul himself? In the final analysis, one will either believe that a scribe "corrected" in this bizarre fashion or else that Paul himself did the "bizarre" thing in the first place. The rest of this analysis will try to give a plausible reason for Paul's being responsible for it.

Is the lectio difficilior impossible for Paul to have written? The answer is no, on two counts. First, one must always be careful about asserting too quickly what an author may or may not have done, especially in matters of style in ad hoc documents. There are just enough instances of unusual word order in this letter to give one reason to pause before announcing that variant 2 is impossible.

Second, and more importantly, both the phrase itself and the word order may significantly reflect the urgency of this letter. Paul's basic problem with this church was their emphasis on being πνευμα-τικοί 'spiritual' and possessing higher σοφία 'wisdom' and γνῶσις 'knowledge', which at the same time had been rather largely divorced from Christian behavior. Part of his own response to this is to describe Christian conversion, as well as community life, with ἅγιος 'holy' words. There are three significant texts in this regard: 1:30, 3:17, 6:11.

In 1:30, in contrast to their enchantment with σοφία and on the basis of what he had earlier said in v. 23, that Christ crucified is God's only wisdom, Paul says again that God has made Christ to become wisdom for us. Ulrich Wilckens and others to the contrary, σοφία is not a christological word,[4] but a soteriological word, as is evidenced by the appositives, δικαιοσύνη 'righteousness/justification', ἁγιασμός 'sanctification' and ἀπολύτρωσις 'redemption'.[5] All of these are soteriological metaphors, and, in the case of the first two, Paul is using metaphors that seem clearly to be moving over into the ethical sphere as well. Thus God made Christ himself to become "sanctification" for them;

---

4. Wilckens (1959: 68–76) sees it in terms of an alleged Gnostic redeemer myth; compare Windisch (1914), who sees it in terms of Jewish speculative wisdom.

5. Thus Paul has moved σοφία from the sphere of philosophy and rhetoric to that of the history of salvation. "Wisdom" is what God has done to effect salvation for his people through the work of Christ.

that is, through him they were saved ("set apart") for God's purposes, to be his holy people in the world.

Likewise in 6:11, when describing how the wicked will not inherit the kingdom, and thereby warning them of the same, he describes their conversion in these terms: "But you were washed, you were sanctified, you were justified," etc. Again, each verb can be shown to be a soteriological metaphor, each appropriate to describe the ethical dimension of the new life that is expected in Christ. You were "washed" from your former wickedness (described in vv. 9–10); you were "set apart" for a life different from before; you were made "right" with God so that you could be "righteous" (δίκαιος) rather than "wicked" (ἄδικοι).

So also 3:17. By their pursuit of wisdom, with its consequent strife over their teachers, they were destroying the church, God's temple in Corinth. In a prophetic word of judgment, Paul announces that God will destroy those who so destroy the church, because his temple is to be ἅγιος 'holy', set apart to be his eschatological people, living out the life of the future in stark contrast to all that was Corinth.

Given this kind of emphasis and usage within the letter, it is not quite precise for Zuntz to suggest that the language οἱ ἡγιασμένοι 'who have been sanctified' is not used by Paul to describe believers. This is in fact thoroughly Pauline language; and in this letter it is crucial language in significant theological texts to describe the believers' new existence in Christ. Thus it should not come as a surprise that this is the first note struck in the salutation. "To the church of God," Paul writes; but before he goes on to locate them geographically, he first describes them in terms of who they are in Christ. Thus, "to the church of God, sanctified in Christ Jesus, which is in Corinth—called to be saints," etc.

Variant 2, therefore, is explicable as a Pauline phenomenon, whereas it is nearly impossible to account for, had Paul actually written variant 1. But if this be the case, then it also presents a special problem for translators. On the one hand, if we follow the ordinary principles of dynamic equivalence and translate as though variant 2 were original after all, we may thereby also eliminate a Pauline emphasis; on the other hand, if we follow Paul's original word order, we end up with a kind of awkwardness that, if left unexplained, leaves the modern reader wondering. I for one would be willing to argue a case for the latter.

1 Corinthians 2:1

The choice here is between μυστήριον 'mystery' (supported by 𝔓⁴⁶ ℵ* A C 88 436 pc a r syᴾ bo Epiph Ambst) and μαρτύριον 'testimony' (supported by B D F G P Ψ 33 81 614 1739 Maj b vg sy^h sa arm). On this variant Metzger (1971: 545) has written:

> From an exegetical point of view the reading μαρτύριον τοῦ θεοῦ, though well supported . . . , is inferior to μυστήριον, which has more limited but early support. . . . The reading μαρτύριον seems to be a recollection of 1.6, whereas μυστήριον here prepares for its usage in ver. 7.

But that will hardly do, since scholarship has been largely divided on this question, and one may read elsewhere (Zuntz 1953: 101):

> The latter assumption [that μαρτύριον is original] can alone account for all the data of the problem. The variant μυστήριον in ii.1 is explicable as being due to assimilation to ii.7.

The questions are two: (1) Did Paul write μυστήριον in anticipation of the argument in vv. 6–16, or did he write μαρτύριον, referring to his preaching as bearing witness to what God had done in Christ crucified? (2) Did a scribe change μυστήριον to μαρτύριον under the influence of 1:6, or μαρτύριον to μυστήριον under the influence of v. 7? Despite the swing of contemporary opinion to the contrary,[6] the evidence seems overwhelmingly in favor of μαρτύριον in answer to these two questions.

On the matter of transcriptional probability, two things need to be noted. First, the two words are so similar that this is less likely a deliberate change as it is a simple case of a scribe's seeing one word and having the other called to mind. The question then is which would be the more common term for a scribe in the early church; that is, which one would he tend automatically to see, no matter which one was before him? A simple glance through Lampe's *Patristic Lexicon* will reveal that the former had become common stock for talking about the gospel, as well as the sacraments, whereas μαρτύριον is seldom so used. It does no good in this regard to appeal to the commonness of the word μάρτυς 'witness' for martyrdom during the second century, since to be a μάρτυς is one thing, but to call the gos-

---

6. Interestingly enough, this is less so in commentaries (Orr and Walther 1976, Mare 1976, and Senft 1979 are exceptions) and translations (GNB and Williams are exceptions), as in a variety of other studies, many of whom, it should be pointed out, have a vested interest in Paul's use of "mystery" language. See, inter alia, Bornkamm 1967: 819; Brown 1968: 48–49; Wilckens 1959: 45; Funk 1966: 295; Schütz 1975: 91; Trites 1977: 203; Kim 1981: 75.

pel itself μαρτύριον 'testimony' is quite another; and the latter simply does not happen in the early church.

Second, both the distance and the relative obscurity of 1:6 make it extremely unlikely that a scribe would recall that text, having μυστήριον before him here, since the scribe himself well knows what is coming in v. 7. But that is what could easily have happened if μαρτύριον were before him. He saw μαρτύριον, but thought μυστήριον, in light of what was about to be said.[7]

The issue of intrinsic probability is more highly subjective in this case, since no one questions whether or not either variant is Pauline. The real question then is the appropriateness of either word at this point in the argument.[8] Metzger and others have argued that μυστήριον here "prepares for its usage in ver. 7." If original, it would surely do so, but the question is whether Paul himself would have done so at this point. The actual flow of Paul's argument suggests otherwise.

Up to this point, and through 2:5, Paul has had a singular concern: to set out in stark contrast his own gospel of Christ crucified over against the self-styled σοφία 'wisdom' of the Corinthians. They are prating wisdom; he is reminding them that the gospel of a crucified Messiah is the divine contradiction to wisdom humanly conceived. Thus in three paragraphs (1:18–25, 1:26–31, 2:1–5) he reminds them of three realities from their original experience of the gospel as Paul preached it that play the lie to their present stance. First, the message itself, with its central focus on Christ crucified (which, he argues, is in fact the true wisdom of God), stands in contradiction to that σοφία (1:18–25); as does, second, the fact that God chose them, not Corinth's beautiful people, to become his people in that city (1:26–31). In this third paragraph Paul now reminds them that when he came among them, his preaching was both materially and formally consonant with such a gospel. The emphasis in this paragraph, therefore, is still on the contradictory nature of the gospel of a crucified Messiah, not on the

7. Zuntz argued that the interchange of χριστοῦ 'Christ' and θεοῦ 'God' in 1:6 is a related matter, which it probably is. That is, the change from the unquestionably original χριστοῦ to θεοῦ was probably influenced by the reading μαρτύριον τοῦ θεοῦ in 2:1. But that admittedly says little as to whether the latter is original here, only that such a text was predominant and influenced the scribe(s) who made this interchange.

8. It is of some interest that scholars on both sides have argued for the appropriateness of either word with καταγγέλλω 'I proclaim'. Findlay (1900: 774), for example, says, "[μαρτύριον] suits better καταγγέλλω," while Bornkamm (1967: 819 n. 141) says, "Since . . . the linking of μαρτύριον with καταγγέλλειν . . . is unusual in the NT, μυστήριον is to be preferred." Bornkamm's is less than impressive argumentation, since μαρτύριον itself as a word for the gospel is rare in the NT (only 1:6, here, and 2 Thess 1:10), and καταγγέλλω is nowhere used with μυστήριον!

heretofore secret nature of that gospel. Just as in 1:6, he is recalling here his original preaching, in which he did not engage in rhetoric and philosophy, but rather bore "witness" to God's saving activity in Christ. In such an argument μαρτύριον is a most appropriate—and natural—expression, while "mystery" would be much less so, since Paul's first preaching was not in terms of revealing God's secret, but of bearing witness to what God had done in Christ.

At v. 6, however, there is a decided turn to the argument. In 1:18–2:5 Paul has twice pointed out that the message of Christ crucified is God's wisdom (1:24, 30), because it was God's power at work doing what worldly σοφία could not, namely bringing salvation to the perishing. In 2:6–16 Paul has two concerns: (1) to point out that the gospel of Christ crucified is recognized as God's wisdom because it has been so revealed by the Spirit, whom we have received; and (2) to nudge them gently to recognize their own inherent contradiction: they think of themselves as πνευματικοί 'spiritual'; Paul's point is that if they truly were so, then they would have recognized that what the Spirit has revealed, namely salvation through the divine contradiction of Christ crucified, is God's wisdom indeed. It is in this context, then, that in v. 7 he now speaks of this wisdom as "hidden," "in mystery," and unknown to the important people of the present age, whom God used to carry out his foreordained plan. God's wisdom can only be known as such by revelation of the Spirit; hence until that revelation it was "in mystery." Thus "mystery" is as appropriate to the argument here as it would have been inappropriate in vv. 1–5.

Finally, it should be noted that the absolute use of μυστήριον as a synonym for the gospel is otherwise unknown in the earlier Paul. The first clear usage is found in Col 1:26–27. This does not mean, of course, that he could not have done so earlier; the question is, given the variety of early uses of this word, whether he did in fact do so. Most likely it is this usage in Colossians that had become so popular in the early church, which, along with the usage in v. 7, caused some early scribes to alter Paul's original μαρτύριον in favor of the more familiar (to them) μυστήριον.

1 Corinthians 2:10

The variant in this case is between δέ 'but' (א A C D F G P Ψ 33 81 Maj latt sy Ephiphanius) and γάρ 'for' ($\mathfrak{P}^{46}$ B 6 365 1175 1739 al Clement Spec). Although the interchange of one conjunctive signal for an-

other may not seem terribly significant for exegesis or translation, here is a case where quite the opposite prevails. One's understanding of both the meaning of v. 9 and its relationship to the rest of the paragraph hinges on this exegetical choice. In fact, a prior commitment to an understanding of that relationship is the only plausible explanation as to how the UBS committee in this instance abandoned its better text-critical judgment for the secondary reading.

Of this interchange Metzger (1971: 546) says: "The loose use of the connective δέ . . . is entirely in Paul's manner, whereas γάρ, though strongly supported . . . , has the appearance of being an improvement introduced by copyists." Zuntz (1953: 205) concurs, adding that "the opposite change, from γάρ to δέ is rare." But in this case these arguments lack force. Indeed, I hope to show that the situation is exactly the opposite of what Metzger has argued.

First, even though the external evidence is basically limited to Egypt, it has the advantage of being the earliest (Clement 𝔓⁴⁶) and best (𝔓⁴⁶ B 1739) of this evidence. Here this external evidence is supported by both transcriptional and intrinsic probabilities, and in this case the questions of Paul's style and intent offer a way through some of the difficulties in understanding this notorious crux.

Despite Metzger and Zuntz to the contrary, transcriptional probabilities are all in favor of γάρ. Except for sheer carelessness, which is not easy to account for (and in any case would favor γάρ over δέ as original),[9] it is difficult to imagine any circumstance under which a scribe, faced with δέ in this text, would have substituted γάρ. This is especially so, since, as the history of translation and interpretation makes plain, an adversative force to this sentence in contrast to "what eye has not seen," etc. in v. 9 seems to make such good sense. On the other hand, for that very reason one can understand how any number of scribes, who failed to make sense of Paul's γάρ, might have expunged it for what seemed to them to be the more natural adversative sense; all the more so, given the fact that the next two sentences also are joined by an explanatory γάρ. Is one to argue that a scribe deliberately created three consecutive uses of γάρ, especially when the first one made such little sense?

Given, then, that γάρ is easily the lectio difficilior and is supported by the best of the Egyptian tradition, can one make sense of it in Paul's argument? An affirmative answer to that question, I hope

9. For the very reason noted in Metzger: that the use of δέ here would be "entirely in Paul's manner," which is why a scribe could have carelessly so conformed it, whereas no amount of carelessness could account for an interchange in the other direction.

to show, not only resolves the textual question, but also offers help for understanding v. 9, which reads literally:

> *But* [ἀλλὰ] even as it stands written:
> (1) What things [ἃ] eye has not seen,
> (2)   and   ear has not heard,
> (3)   and has not entered into the heart of man
> (4) What things [ἃ] God has prepared for those who love him
>   *for* [γὰρ] or *but* [δὲ]
>   to us God has revealed through the Spirit.

Besides the question of the source of the quotation, which does not concern us here, there are two basic problems with this verse. (1) The sentence itself is an anacolouthon; the problem has to do with the double ἃ 'what things', and how one is going to understand what Paul intended to be the subject and object of the sentence. (2) How does the quotation function in the argument itself? Is it the conclusion of vv. 6–8, or does it begin a new direction to the argument? On these matters interpreters and English translations differ considerably.

With regard to the first item there are basically three options. (*a*) Omit the first ἃ and translate the second as 'what', so that line 4 functions as the object of the three verbs in lines 1–3 (NIV: "No eye has seen, no ear has heard, no mind has conceived what God has prepared for those who love him"; compare NAB and Montgomery). (*b*) The opposite of that: Omit ἃ in line 4, so that lines 1–3 function as the object of the verb "has prepared" in line 4 (GNB: "What no one ever saw or heard, what no one ever thought could happen, is the very thing God prepared for those who love him"). (*c*) Make both occurrences of ἃ coordinate and the whole of the quotation function as the object of the verb ἀπεκάλυψεν 'has revealed' in v. 10 (RSV: "What no eye has seen, nor ear heard, nor the heart of man conceived, what God has prepared for those who love him, God has revealed to us through the Spirit"; compare NEB).[10] These latter assume a text with δέ, but then proceed to run roughshod over it, as if conjunctive signals were irrelevant.

The second question gets equally diverse treatment. (*a*) Some avoid the question by simply translating all of vv. 6–16 as a single

10. JB has taken the opposite stance of this one, by reworking the introductory formula so that the quotation becomes the object of γέγραπται 'it is written' ("We teach what scripture calls: the things that no eye has seen and no ear has heard, things beyond the mind of man, all that God has prepared for those who love him").

paragraph—which it is, but one cannot thereby tell how v. 9 functions in the argument. (*b*) NIV and NEB see the first subparagraph to be vv. 6–10a. In the scheme of NIV, v. 9 is adversative to vv. 6–8 ("however"), although it is not at all clear how so; in the scheme of NEB, v. 9 is also adversative to vv. 6–8, but because they treat it as part of v. 10a, the whole of vv. 9–10a expresses the revelatory character of what the "rulers" did not understand. (*c*) By adding a comma after the strong adversative (ἀλλά) that begins v. 9, RSV and GNB take this verse to begin a new subparagraph (RSV: "But, as it is written," etc.). This comes out at the same place as NEB, even though the paragraphing is different. That is, in all such cases, even though the quotation in v. 9 touches on the subject matter of vv. 6–8, its real role is to set up the contrast that begins the new subject matter of vv. 10–13.

I would like to suggest another alternative, which sees γάρ in v. 10 as intentional on Paul's part and therefore as an integral part of his argumentation.[11]

First, although it will not be argued for here, the linguistic and contextual evidence overwhelmingly favors "the rulers of this age" as referring to the human rulers responsible for the death of Jesus,[12] who thereby also represent for Paul the "leaders" in terms of σοφία that is merely of this age. Thus he sets them up as those who represent the σοφοί ("wise") whom the Corinthians would now emulate in their feverish pursuit of σοφία.

Second, the stylistic clue to this passage lies with the introductory formula, ἀλλὰ καθὼς γέγραπται 'but even as it stands written'. Most translations take this to be an independent clause, the whole of which is adversative-supportive of vv. 6–8. This exact formula, however, appears two other times in Paul, in Rom 15:3–4 and 15:20–21, and in both cases ἀλλά 'but' functions with the preceding sentence, as part of an οὐ/ἀλλά 'not/but' contrast. Thus:

Rom 15:3–4:   For Christ did *not . . . But* as it is written . . .
      15:20–21:   . . . so that I would *not . . . but* just as it is written . . .

---

11. Frid (1985) offers a slightly different solution, which has a similar net result. He sees the sentence in v. 9 as elliptical and would add the verb "we know" from v. 8. Thus: "None of them knew, but, as it is written, what things . . . , these things we do know."

12. The oft-repeated assertion that this term refers to demonic powers, either on their own or behind the earthly rulers, needs to be laid to rest. The linguistic evidence is decisive: (1) the term ἄρχοντες 'rulers' is never equated with the ἀρχαί 'principalities'

It should also be noted that in the case of 15:3, the succeeding sentence is connected with γάρ and is clearly explanatory of the citation. This stylistic feature suggests (*a*) that v. 9 is intended to provide support for vv. 6–8, as the adversative to the negatives in v. 8 ("The rulers did *not* understand, for if they had, they would *not* have crucified the Lord of glory, *but* . . . "); (*b*) that v. 9 thus belongs with vv. 6–8, which together form the first subparagraph of the argument; and (*c*) v. 10 therefore begins a new subparagraph by means of an explanation of v. 9.

Third, the argument of vv. 6–9, therefore, goes something like this. In v. 6 Paul has argued that, despite his pejorative treatment of wisdom in 1:17–2:5, there is nonetheless true σοφία for the believer (God's σοφία), which is not available to the leaders of the present age—because they pursue wisdom that is merely human (of this world, of this age). The divine σοφία, he goes on to explain in vv. 7–8, which was held "in mystery" and "once hidden" in God, was destined by God for our glory. Such wisdom, Paul repeats in v. 8, was not known by those who thought they had wisdom. That he intends nothing new or esoteric here is demonstrated by the next clause: *had* they known this hidden wisdom, they would *not* have crucified the Lord of glory. That is, divine wisdom is once more joined to Jesus Christ and him crucified, as in 1:23, 1:30, and 2:2. Right at this point, he adds a contrast: "But even as it stands written." Thus: "Had they known, they would *not* have crucified him, *but* as it is written, what things eye has not seen," etc.

Fourth, this leads, then, to some clues about the structure of the quotation. First, the two parts of the quotation, lines 1–3 and 4, support the two emphases in vv. 6–8. Lines 1–3 correspond to the rulers who did not understand, for if they had they would not have crucified Christ (note especially line 3, "the heart of ἀνθρώπου [man] has not conceived"); line 4 corresponds to "what God has determined from before the ages for our glory." Second, since the quota-

---

of Col 1:16 and Eph 6:12; (2) when ἄρχων 'leader' appears in the singular it sometimes refers to Satan; but (3) there is no evidence of any kind, either in Jewish or Christian writings until the second century, that the term was used of demons; furthermore, (4) in the NT in the plural it invariably refers to earthly rulers and unambiguously does so in Paul in Rom 13:3; and (5) it is used regularly by Luke to refer to those responsible for the death of Jesus. It has been argued that the case for demonic powers rests on the addition "of this age," as in the singular "ruler of this world" in Eph 2:2 (cf. John 12:31). But that still will not work in this case, since the phrase *of this age* comes directly from 1:20–21, where the Jewish expert in the law and the Greek philosopher are further styled "the disputer of this age."

tion functions as a contrast to the rulers of this age, its whole point aims at line 4: what God has prepared for those who *love* him. Third, since the aim of the quotation is line 4, this suggests that both occurrences of ἅ be understood in a way similar to Moffatt's translation, where the second ἅ functions something like ταῦτα 'these things'. This means that the second ἅ is best understood as in apposition to the first and that both function as the object of the verb "has prepared." Thus: "What eye has not seen, and ear has not heard, and the heart of man has not conceived, these things God has prepared for those who love him." Therefore, even though it gives scriptural support for the lack of understanding by the rulers of this age, the quotation also picks up the motif of those who do understand. What Paul will now go on to explain in v. 10 is how we understand, the key to which of course is the Spirit.

How then does v. 10 function? Given the stylistic feature of Rom 15:3–4, v. 10a begins the new subparagraph that gets to the point of the whole section—our being able to understand what the rulers could not, because we have the Spirit while they do not. The first three sentences begin with an explanatory γάρ, each of which explains the former sentence.[13]

For to us God has revealed by his Spirit;
  for the Spirit searches all things, even the depths of God;
    for [by way of analogy] who knows the mind of man, etc.

The first γάρ functions as the explanatory conjunction to the quotation in v. 9, especially as it climaxes with line 4. Thus Paul says, "What things were not formerly known are the things that God has prepared for those of us who love him; *for* to us God has revealed them by his Spirit." In this view, not only is sense made of the lectio difficilior of v. 10, but also v. 9 is placed in its proper role in the argument, both to bring support and closure to vv. 6–8, as well as to lead into vv. 10–13.

I trust that these brief exercises in textual criticism, as it impacts exegesis and translation, will not only be an honor to Dr. Greenlee, but will also help us better to understand God's Word, to which task all of Dr. Greenlee's academic labors have been devoted.

---

13. This compounding of explanatory γάρ is a unique feature of 1 Corinthians (see, e.g., 1:18–21, 3:2–4, 4:15, and 9:15–16).

References

Bornkamm, G.
1967 "μυστήριον." Vol. 4: pp. 802–27 in *Theological Dictionary of the New Testament.* Edited by Gerhard Kittel and Gerhard Friedrich. Grand Rapids: Eerdmans.

Brown, Raymond E.
1968 *The Semitic Background of the Term "Mystery" in the New Testament.* Philadelphia: Fortress.

Fee, Gordon D.
1987 *The First Epistle to the Corinthians.* New International Commentary on the New Testament. Grand Rapids: Eerdmans.

Findlay, G. G.
1900 "St. Paul's First Epistle to the Corinthians." Vol. 2: pp. 727–953 in *The Expositor's Greek Testament.* Edited by W. Robertson Nicoll. London: Hodder & Stoughton.

Frid, Bo
1985 "The Enigmatic ΑΛΛΑ in I Corinthians 2.9." *New Testament Studies* 31:603–11.

Funk, Robert W.
1966 "Word and Word in 1 Corinthians 2:6–16." Pp. 275–305 in *Language, Hermeneutic, and Word of God.* New York: Harper & Row.

Kim, Seyoon
1981 *The Origin of Paul's Gospel.* Tübingen: Mohr.

Mare, W. Harold.
1976 "1 Corinthians." Vol. 10: pp. 173–297 in *The Expositor's Bible Commentary.* Edited by Frank E. Gaebelein. Grand Rapids: Zondervan.

Metzger, Bruce M.
1971 *A Textual Commentary on the Greek New Testament.* London: United Bible Societies.

Orr, William F., and James Arthur Walther
1976 *I Corinthians.* Anchor Bible. Garden City: Doubleday.

Schütz, John H.
1975 *Paul and the Anatomy of Apostolic Authority.* Cambridge: Cambridge University Press.

Senft, Christophe
1979 *La Première Épître de Saint-Paul aux Corinthiens.* Neuchâtel: Delachaux & Nestle.

Trites, Allison A.
1977 *The New Testament Concept of Witness.* Cambridge: Cambridge University Press.

Wilckens, Ulrich
1959 *Weisheit und Torheit.* Tübingen: Mohr.

Windisch, Hans
    1914   "Die göttliche Weisheit der Juden und die paulinische
            Christologie." Pp. 220–34 in *Neutestamentliche Studien: Georg
            Heinrici zu seinem 70. Geburtstag*. Edited by Hans Windisch.
            Leipzig: Hinrichs.
Zuntz, Günther
    1953   *The Text of the Epistles*. Schweich Lectures 1946. London: Oxford
            University Press for the British Academy.

The Text of Galatians: Evidence from the Earliest Greek Manuscripts

Moisés Silva

Westminster Theological Seminary

It is worthy of note that, among the various introductions to the textual criticism of the NT, Dr. Greenlee's work is the only one that devotes a separate chapter to manuscript collation (Greenlee 1964: chap. 9). Though tedious and difficult, the task of collating NT manuscripts can be exceptionally rewarding. Students and even scholars may be tempted to think of such work as supererogatory; after all, are not the variants to be culled from the important documents readily available? Only a few hours spent carefully analyzing a Greek manuscript should dispel this illusion—and it would also prevent a number of irrelevant (and sometimes incorrect) comments found here and there among the commentaries.

The present article is a modest contribution intended to show the value of fresh collations and thus to encourage others to undertake similar projects. My project here is narrowly circumscribed: it focuses on only one brief NT book, and it examines only those Greek manuscripts dated to the fifth century or earlier: Papyrus 46 and codexes

17

Vaticanus, Sinaiticus, and Alexandrinus (excluded are a few early but fragmentary documents, such as Papyrus 51 and Codex Ephraimi). On the other hand, the collations are truly exhaustive in character, even to the smallest orthographic detail. Most spelling variations, as well as singular readings that are obvious scribal errors, have no direct value either for the establishment of the text or for the (genealogical) reconstruction of its history. They are of great value, however, for determining scribal tendencies, a knowledge of which is essential when making a judgment on other, more substantive variations.

The most common collation base (that is, the text against which the manuscripts are examined) is the Textus Receptus. While there are good reasons for that choice, the goal in this paper is to determine, at least in broad strokes, the ways in which the Greek manuscripts depart from the original. Since we do not possess the autograph, our only reasonable choice is the text adopted by the United Bible Societies (UBS[3] = NA[26]). Though no one is likely to equate this text fully with the original, few knowledgeable scholars would deny that it is a very close approximation to it—certainly closer to the NT autograph than modern editions of other Greek writings are to their respective autographs, and no doubt close enough to provide us with statistically reliable data. In other words, even though occasional readings treated here as variants from the original may in fact constitute the original readings, the textual profile reflected in the totals is unlikely to mislead us (indeed, such a profile would perhaps not vary substantially regardless of the collation base used).

Papyrus 46

The significance of $\mathfrak{P}^{46}$ from the Chester Beatty collection can hardly be overestimated. Dated with confidence about A.D. 200, it provides what is by far the earliest nearly complete text of Galatians (because of erosion at the bottom of each leaf, the following verses are missing: 1:8b–10a, 2:10–12a, 3:15b–16a, 3:29b–4:2a, 4:17b–19, 4:31b–5:2a). The scribe, to be sure, must be characterized as somewhat careless, but most of his errors are of the self-correcting kind, and thus his basic underlying text (almost universally regarded as of the highest quality) is easily recovered. (For an authoritative description of this manuscript, see Kenyon 1936–37; for a superb analysis of its textual character, see Zuntz 1953, which focuses on 1 Corinthians and Hebrews; for the most recent and thorough discussion of the scribe's habits, based on singular readings, see Royse 1981.)

The total number of variations comes to 136, but 44 of them consist of orthographic differences that have no intrinsic significance, and so we can dismiss them from further discussion except to note two matters. A full 17 of these differences are cases of itacism, in particular the use of the diphthong ει where the UBS³ text has ι (in 1:6 the papyrus has ημας instead of υμας, but this variant should probably not be classified as orthographic). One should also note that there are no interchanges between ε and αι or between ο and ω.

Among the nonorthographic variants, we should note a large number of omissions, namely 39 (9 of which involve more than one word), in contrast to only 5 (minor) additions, so that the text of Galatians in this papyrus is about 45 words shorter than the UBS³ text. More than half of the omissions, incidentally, involve "function" words, such as prepositions, articles, and conjunctions, whereas single verbs are never omitted. Significant omissions include the clause και καλεσας δια της χαριτος αυτου in 1:15; ο συν εμοι in 2:3 (a singular reading not noted in NA²⁶); και ουχι ιουδαικως in 2:14; χαριν προσετεθη in 3:19; του υιου in 4:6 (supported by Marcion, according to Tertullian); and ουδε εξεπτυσατε in 4:14 (singular).

Another 29 variants consist of grammatical changes, all but three of which involve verbal endings (e.g., 1:16, ευαγγελισομαι rather than -ζωμαι; 2:12, ηλθεν rather than -ον). The rest of the variants involve word order (e.g., 3:8, τα εθνη δικαιοι rather than δικαιοι τα εθνη), the use of equivalent terms (1:4, περι rather than υπερ; 2:9, πετρος rather than κηφας; 4:31, αρα rather than διο), and other changes more difficult to classify. Among the latter, some are simply careless mistakes that yield nonsense (e.g., οθεν for το ευαγγελισθεν in 1:11), while others consist of interesting singular readings, such as ουκετι for ουκ ενι in 3:28 and αρα for οφελον in 5:12.

Codex Sinaiticus

The three scribes who produced Codex Sinaiticus in the middle of the fourth century evidently belonged to a well-trained professional class. In comparison with $\mathfrak{P}^{46}$, their handwriting is more beautiful and uniform. The Pauline epistles were copied by a scribe identified as A, possibly the best of the three, though he was certainly not faultless. (The latest thorough discussion of this manuscript is Milne and Skeat 1938.)

The total number of variations is 130, in comparison with 136 for $\mathfrak{P}^{46}$, but this similarity is quite misleading, since fully 81 of these variations are orthographic. About 50 of them consist of ι for ει; another dozen reflect the confusion between ε and αι (only one possible instance of o/ω, 1:1, αυτων for αυτον, but note below regarding 6:9–10). The interchange between ε and αι is of special interest, because Codex Sinaiticus is listed in the apparatus of NA²⁶ at 4:18 as supporting the infinitive ζηλουσθαι; in fact, it is probable that the scribe meant the indicative ζηλουσθε (cf. in the same context ηδικησαται, v. 12, and οιδαται, v. 13, both for -τε).

In any case, only 49 variants (in comparison with 92 for 𝔓⁴⁶) may be considered substantive. Omissions account for 16 of the variations (8 of them involving function words) and additions for 6. Only a few other types of variants have affected the length of the text. As a result (and in great contrast to 𝔓⁴⁶), Galatians in Codex Sinaiticus is only 14 words shorter than UBS³—and if we leave out of account the 8-word omission at 2:8, from ο γαρ το περιτομης (a clear example of homoeoteleuton, since v. 7 ends with περιτομης), the difference in length becomes almost immaterial. Interesting omissions are παυλος in 5:2 and οτι in 5:3.

Variants involving some kind of morphological change are 14 in number. Particularly interesting are the hortatory subjunctives θερισωμεν and εχωμεν in 6:9–10, where UBS³ has indicatives. Other notable variants are ειπον instead of προειπον in 5:21 and the transposition τα εθνη δικαιοι in 3:8 (in common with 𝔓⁴⁶).

Codex Vaticanus

Moving to a collation of Codex Vaticanus is like a breath of fresh air, since the scribe responsible for the NT was much more competent and careful than the ones we have already looked at. Even this scribe, to be sure, is not immune to making careless mistakes. Indeed, one of the most infamous mistakes among early NT manuscripts occurs here at 1:11, where the text should read το ευαγγελιον το ευαγγελισθεν υπ᾽ εμου 'the gospel that was preached by me'. After the scribe wrote the first two words of this phrase, however, fatigue or daydreaming must have overcome him, for he repeated those two words—not once but twice!—before proceeding: το ευαγγελιον το ευαγγελιον το ευαγγελιον το ευαγγελισθεν υπ᾽ εμου.

This amusing example is all the more notable in that the rest of the epistle is so carefully done. My collation yielded a total of only 67 variations, almost half of them orthographic in character. The sharp decrease in the number of nonorthographic variants from 92 in 𝔓⁴⁶ to 37

in Vaticanus (similarly 40 in Alexandrinus; Sinaiticus holds an inter-
mediary position with 49) is perhaps indicative of the growing skills
among professional biblical scribes in the early centuries of the Christian era.

Apart from the problem at 1:11, we find only 3 additions (2 articles
and 1 preposition), while omissions total 13 instances: the text is only
6 words shorter than that of UBS³. The omissions deserve special attention, however. Half of them involve function words (the same proportion in 𝔓⁴⁶), but another five affect divine names: ο θεος in 1:15 and
4:6, του θεου in 3:21, ιησου in 5:6, and εν κυριω in 5:10. Since omissions
of divine names account for only 4 out of 33 total omissions in 𝔓⁴⁶,
and since Sinaiticus never omits a divine name in Galatians, this feature of Vaticanus ought to play a more significant role than it has in
text-critical decisions. The point is confirmed when we note that of
the 5 omissions in question, 2 of them (5:6 and 10) are unsupported by
any other Greek manuscript (though Tischendorf cites slight, and
probably misleading, patristic support) and 2 others (3:21 and 4:6) by
only one Greek manuscript each (𝔓⁴⁶ and 1739, respectively, plus very
slight versional evidence).

Among other types of variants, it is also noteworthy that Vaticanus
has 5 transpositions—about the same number as (and therefore a
higher proportion than) the other two manuscripts. Significantly, 3 of
them (as opposed to only 1 in 𝔓⁴⁶ and Sinaiticus) involve the divine
name Jesus Christ: 2:16 (twice) and 3:14. The UBS³ text has wisely not
followed Vaticanus in these instances. Finally, it is of some grammatical
interest to note that twice Vaticanus replaces εαν with αν (5:17 and 6:7),
while at 3:19 αν takes the place of ου (οὖ).

Codex Alexandrinus

Dating to the fifth century, Codex Alexandrinus rivals Vaticanus in
the care with which it was produced. Though the total number of
variations is just over 100, a full 65 of them are orthographic in
character (24 = ι/ει; 26 = ε/αι). The number of remaining substantive
variations is therefore almost identical with that found in Vaticanus.
The kinds of variants found, however, differ in one important respect. While the ratio of additions to omissions is 4 : 13 in Vaticanus,
it is 11 : 4 in Alexandrinus. This piece of information suggests that
the scribe of Alexandrinus was more careful than that of Vaticanus
in avoiding thoughtless omissions; indeed, only the article τη in 5:7

and the conjunction δε in 2:16 probably belong in this category (the omission of και κηφας in 2:9 and of the third occurrence of ζω in 2:20 could possibly be explained as deliberate).

Of the 11 additions, 4 are relatively insignificant, but the others are quite interesting. For example, Alexandrinus is the earliest Greek manuscript that adds φονοι 'murder' to the list of the works of the flesh in 5:21. The other 4 instances were motivated by the desire to harmonize the text with a parallel passage: in 3:5 το πνευμα ελαβετε is added after νομου in harmony with v. 2; the word ταυτην is added to 4:30 in conformity with the LXX text being quoted; the expression του σταυρου in 5:11 becomes του σταυρου του χριστου (cf. 6:12, 14; 1 Cor 1:7; Phil 3:18); and the phrase εν χριστω ιησου, original in 5:6, is added to the parallel passage 6:15.

The ratio of additions to omissions in Alexandrinus contributes to the fact that this is the earliest Greek manuscript whose text of Galatians is actually longer (by 9 words) than that of UBS[3].

Agreements among the Manuscripts

Considering the total number of variants involved, one is surprised to find that there is not one instance in which all four manuscripts—which are supposed to belong to an "Alexandrian" family broadly defined—agree against UBS[3]. Moreover, there are only a few instances where three of the manuscripts agree against UBS[3]:

𝔓[46]=Vat.=Alex.: 0
𝔓[46]=Vat.=Sin.: 1 (2:12, ηλθεν for ηλθον)
𝔓[46]=Sin.=Alex.: 2 (1:4, περι for υπερ; 1:11, δε for γαρ)
Vat.=Sin.=Alex.: 1 (5:7, omission of τη)

Agreements between any two manuscripts vary widely. We find only a few agreements between the following:

Vat.=Alex.: 3
Vat.=Sin.: 5
𝔓[46]=Alex.: 4
𝔓[46]=Sin.: 5

On the other hand, there appears to be a significantly large number of agreements in the following two sets:

𝔓[46]=Vat.: 10
Sin.=Alex.: 10

Implications

Since the data summarized above is very small, it would be unwise to draw firm conclusions. The material does have implications, however, for our evaluation and use of NT manuscripts.

Implications for specific manuscripts. Since many of the variants exhibited by any manuscript reflect the copy from which a scribe is working rather than the scribe's own errors, my figures cannot give a completely accurate profile of individual scribal habits. For that purpose, it would be much better to record only singular readings (cf. Royse 1981: chap. 1). On the other hand, if we want to know the profile of the manuscript (which includes the variations introduced by its scribe as well as the ones he simply transfers from his master copy), all of the variants should be taken into account.

A brief look at table 1 should make it clear that scribal tendencies are not completely uniform. While the percentage of variants that involve grammatical changes (= number of grammatical changes divided by number of variants in each manuscript) is basically the same for all four manuscripts (24%–30%), we have already noted that Alexandrinus has a significantly lower percentage of omissions (10%) than the other three manuscripts (30%–35%). Conversely, Alexandrinus has approximately twice as many additions as the others. As mentioned earlier, Vaticanus has a disproportionately large number of variations that involve the divine names, while Alexandrinus tends to harmonize on the basis of parallel passages. Clearly, responsible text-critical decisions cannot be made without some knowledge of the individual characteristics of the witnesses being used.

Implications for scribal habits generally. There has been a good deal of discussion over the years regarding the principle that "the shorter reading is better." In particular, Royse (1981: 2–3) has argued that for the early period of the papyri, that principle does not work. At first blush it may appear that my figures support Royse. In fact, however, the old principle is still valid as long as we keep in mind that its proponents (especially Griesbach) qualified it carefully by excepting certain variants, such as those small and unimportant words that are easily missed and those that could be explained by homoeoteleuton (I have argued this point in Silva 1985). It is true the $\mathfrak{P}^{46}$ has a much larger number of omissions than additions (35 : 5), but most of the omissions indeed involve function words or are the result of homoeoteleuton. Particularly worthy of note in this connection is the fact that among all of the omissions in the four manuscripts only one involves a verb (ζω in Alexandrinus at 2:20, where the verb had already appeared twice).

TABLE 1. *Statistical table of manuscript collation in Galatians*

	$\mathfrak{P}^{46}$	Sinaiticus	Vaticanus	Alexandrinus
ADDITIONS				
FU	2	3	3	4
NO	2	3	1	6
VB	1	0	0	0
PH	0	0	0	1
Subtotal	5	6	4	11
OMISSIONS				
FU	18	6	7	2
NO	9	6	6	0
VB	0	0	0	1
PH	6	3	0	1
Subtotal	33	15	13	4
EQUIVALENT (one-to-one changes)				
FU	8	5	5	7
NO	6	1	0	2
VB	0	0	0	1
PH	2	0	0	0
Subtotal	16	6	5	10
GRAMMATICAL				
FU	2	0	0	0
NO	4	4	2	1
VB	22	10	7	9
PH	0	0	0	0
Subtotal	28	14	9	10
TRANSPOSITIONS				
NO (Divine)	1	1	3	1
PH	3	4	2	3
Subtotal	4	5	5	4
MISCELLANEOUS				
FU	0	0	0	0
NO	2	1	1	0
VB	1	2	0	0
PH	3	0	0	1
Subtotal	6	3	1	1
TOTAL	92	49	37	40

Key

FU   function words
NO   nominal forms, including modifiers and divine-name combinations
VB   verbal forms
PH   phrases, except for divine name combinations

Implications for genealogical relationships. My evidence does not lend itself easily to genealogical analysis, for which variants need to be selected carefully. As suggested above, however, the absence of variants in which all four manuscripts agree against UBS[3] raises questions about the supposed "Alexandrian" text-type. One could argue that the UBS[3] text itself, by depending heavily on the Alexandrian text-type, has already assimilated the distinctives of the manuscripts in question. But that consideration is not fully persuasive. A common genetic relationship can only be demonstrated through commonality of errors. If we assume that the UBS[3] text reflects fairly accurately the original, then we must concede that at least the text of Galatians reveals no special relationship among these four manuscripts. It would be unwise, however, to extrapolate from Galatians to the whole Pauline corpus. The real significance of the data presented in this article can only surface when a more sophisticated and wide-ranging investigation is conducted (cf. especially the model provided by Zuntz 1953).

References

Greenlee, J. Harold
  1964   *Introduction to New Testament Textual Criticism.* Grand Rapids: Eerdmans.
Kenyon, Frederic G.
  1936–37 *The Chester Beatty Biblical Papyri: Descriptions and Texts of Twelve Manuscripts on Papyrus of the Greek Bible* 3: *Supplement: Pauline Epistles.* 2 vols. London: Emery Walker.
Milne, H. J. M., and T. C. Skeat
  1938   *Scribes and Correctors of the Codex Sinaiticus.* London: British Museum.
Royse, James Ronald
  1981   *Scribal Habits in Early Greek New Testament Papyri.* Th.D. diss., Graduate Theological Union, Berkeley.
Silva, Moisés
  1985   "Internal evidence in the text-critical use of the LXX." Pp. 151–67 in *La Septuaginta en la investigación contemporánea.* Edited by N. Fernández Marcos. Madrid: C.S.I.C.
Zuntz, Günther
  1953   *The Text of the Epistles: A Disquisition upon the corpus Paulinum.* Schweich Lectures 1946. London: Oxford University Press for British Academy.

Textual Problems in the Epistle to the Hebrews

F. F. Bruce†

University of Manchester

The text of the Epistle to the Hebrews has been transmitted since the early second century as part of the *corpus Paulinum*. The earliest extant copy of the epistle belongs to the earliest extant copy of the corpus, $\mathfrak{P}^{46}$ (ca. A.D. 200), where it appears between Romans and 1 Corinthians. At what point in the second century Hebrews was first included in the corpus cannot be determined. One scholar indeed has argued that it was in the corpus from the beginning (Anderson 1966); Zuntz, however (1953: 15–16), had already shown adequate reason to believe that this cannot have been so, since Christian writers early in the second century who apparently knew the Pauline corpus as such betray no acquaintance with Hebrews. That all surviving copies of Hebrews go back to one archetype, the edition which was originally admitted to the Pauline corpus, is suggested by their having a number of errors in common, including a few primitive corruptions which were taken over into the corpus.

The text of the twelve passages discussed below is taken from UBS[3]; at the head of each discussion this text is reproduced with its principal witnesses, followed by one or more variant readings with their principal witnesses.

Hebrews 2:9

ὅπως χάριτι θεοῦ ὑπὲρ παντὸς γεύσηται θανάτου

    χάριτι θεοῦ   𝔓⁴⁶ ℵ A B C D K P Ψ *Byz* lat syr cop arm eth

    χωρὶς θεοῦ   0121b 424** 1739* lat^vg.g syr^pesh.codd Orig^pt Euseb

    Ambst Ambr *al*

χάριτι θεοῦ is far and away the majority reading, but the variant χωρὶς θεοῦ is attested by an impressive range of witnesses, both East and West, including manuscripts known to Origen, Ambrose, and Jerome, together with the Greek fathers Theodore, Theodoret, Anastasius of Sinai, Ps.-Oecumenius, and Theophylact, and the Latin fathers Fulgentius and Vigilius (in addition to the fathers cited above).

"By the grace of God" makes excellent sense in the context, but "apart from God" is such a striking variant, and so widely attested, that one wonders if the precept *praestat lectio ardua* is not applicable here. It is most improbable that χάριτι θεοῦ should have been corrupted or otherwise changed to χωρὶς θεοῦ. But do the words *in order that he, apart from God, should taste death for everyone* make any sense in the context? Bengel (1734: ad loc.) thought they did: he construed χωρὶς θεοῦ with ὑπὲρ παντός to yield "Christ tasted death for everyone apart from God." Zuntz (1953: 34–35, 43–45), who reads δι' ἑαυτοῦ in Heb 1:3 (following 𝔓⁴⁶ and 1739) and interprets it to mean that Christ effected purification from sins "by his own virtue and effort, with no assistance from outside" (not even from God), takes χωρὶς θεοῦ in a similar sense: "Textual criticism thus brings out a neglected aspect of the theology of Hebrews." He agrees with Harnack (1929: 63) that objections to χωρὶς θεοῦ in this sense led to the "dogmatic correction" to χάριτι θεοῦ.

I am disposed to agree that χάριτι θεοῦ was an early correction of χωρὶς θεοῦ but that χωρὶς θεοῦ was not part of the original text of Hebrews. It was first introduced, probably, as a marginal gloss against Heb 2:8, where Ps 8:6 is quoted to the effect that God has subjected everything to the "son of man." The glossator intended "apart from God" to qualify "everything"—"everything, that is to say, apart from God himself." In adding this qualification he followed the precedent of Paul who, quoting the same psalm in 1 Cor 15:27b, points out that the statement *everything has been subjected to him* self-evidently excludes the one who subjected everything to him. In due course the marginal gloss was introduced into the text at a point where the scribe thought it appropriate—in Heb 2:9. If that is so, the original wording of the clause was "in order that he should taste death for everyone." The scribe probably supposed, as Bengel did, that χωρὶς θεοῦ could qualify ὑπὲρ παντός, but in that case it would have followed ὑπὲρ παντός instead of preceding it. Metzger (1971: 664) suggests that the scribe who incorporated χωρὶς θεοῦ into the text did so because he thought χωρίς was intended to be a correction of χάριτι. But it seems more likely to me that χάριτι θεοῦ was not originally in the text but was the emendation of a second scribe who could make no sense of χωρὶς θεοῦ in the context.

Hebrews 3:6

ἐάν (περ) τὴν παρρησίαν καὶ τὸ καύχημα τῆς ἐλπίδος κατάσχωμεν

    κατάσχωμεν   𝔓¹³ 𝔓⁴⁶ B Ψ copˢᵃʰ ethʳᵒ Lucif Ambr

    μέχρι τέλους βεβαίαν κατάσχωμεν   ℵ A C D K P 0121b 33 1739
        1881 2495 *Byz* lat syrʰᶜˡ ᵖᵃˡ copᵇᵒʰ arm eth *al*

On the face of it there is something strange about the feminine βεβαίαν. We should expect the neuter βέβαιον in agreement with καύχημα. While βεβαίαν might be taken to agree with παρρησίαν, it would be unnatural to have the adjective agreeing with the more remote rather than with the nearer noun. It is almost certain that the words μέχρι τέλους βεβαίαν were imported from the similarly constructed v. 14, ἐάνπερ τὴν ἀρχὴν τῆς ὑποστάσεως μέχρι τέλους βεβαίαν κατάσχωμεν, where the feminine adjective is naturally construed with ἀρχήν.

Hebrews 4:2

ἀλλ᾽ οὐκ ὠφέλησεν ὁ λόγος τῆς ἀκοῆς ἐκείνους μὴ συγκεκερασμένους τῇ πίστει τοῖς ἀκούσασιν

    συγκεκερασμένους   𝔓¹³ 𝔓⁴⁶ A B C D* Ψ 0121b *al* (with the synonymous συγκεκραμένους in Dᶜ K P ᵐⁱⁿⁿ·ᵖˡ)

    συγκεκερασμένος   ℵ Eph Cyrᵖᵗ Theodoret

The author reminds his readers that he and they have had the gospel preached to them, just as the Israelites of the wilderness generation had, "but the word of hearing did not profit them, because they were not united by faith with those who had heard." This is the rendering of the British Revised Version (1881), following the reading which is now preferred by UBS³. Certainly this is the majority reading, but it is hard to make sense of it. "They" to whom the gospel was preached in the wilderness generation were themselves the hearers: how then could it be said that they were "not united by faith with those who heard"?

William Manson (1951: 58) took the majority reading to mean that "the Christian Group at Rome whom the author addresses was separating itself in the matter of 'faith' from the true believing body of the Church." This might indeed have been so with the people to whom the letter is addressed; but the author makes the statement with regard to the Israelites of the wilderness generation, and to them this interpretation is inapplicable.

The majority reading is the earliest attested reading; it is, moreover, the reading which best explains the variants. It is difficult to avoid the conclusion that Zuntz is right in treating those variants as so many "ancient conjectures vainly striving to heal a primitive corruption" (1953: 16).

One variant replaces the active participle ἀκούσασιν with the passive ἀκουσθεῖσιν (attested by Theodore of Mopsuestia): "Because they were not united by faith with the things they heard." Other witnesses (D* 104 1611 2495 syr^{hcl,mg} Lucif al) replace the dative with the genitive τῶν ἀκουσάντων, but this makes sense only if the accusative plural συγκεκερασμένους be replaced by the nominative singular συγκεκερασμένος (in concord with λόγος). The nominative singular is indeed read, as has been said above, by א and some other witnesses. As it stands in these manuscripts and versions, συγκεκερασμένος is probably a conjectural emendation: if so, the conjecture was a happy one. Whoever first thought of mending the text in this way did not strive so "vainly" as Zuntz suggests: the original text may well have been restored by accident. RSV, like several other modern versions, follows this minority reading in its rendering: "The message which they heard did not benefit them, because it did not meet with faith in the hearers."

Hebrews 6:2

μὴ πάλιν θεμέλιον καταβαλλόμενοι . . . βαπτισμῶν διδαχῆς
    διδαχῆς   א A C D I K P 0122 Byz lat^{vg} syr^{hcl} arm
    διδαχήν   𝔓^{46} B lat^d syr^{pesh}

Alexandrian, "Western," and Byzantine witnesses combine impressively to attest the genitive διδαχῆς. "Let us go on to perfection," says the author, "not laying again a foundation of repentance from dead works and of faith toward God. . . . " Does he then continue with "of teaching [διδαχῆς] about ablutions" or with "teaching [διδαχήν] about ablutions"? If διδαχῆς is read, it is one of a series of genitives all dependent on θεμέλιον and indicating what the foundation consists of. If διδαχήν is read, it is in apposition to θεμέλιον, and the genitives which follow are (like βαπτισμῶν) dependent on διδαχήν, not on θεμέλιον—"teaching about ablutions and the imposition of hands, about resurrection of the dead and final judgment." Although διδαχήν is so sparsely attested in comparison with διδαχῆς, it has serious claims to be recognized as the original reading. It is difficult to see why διδαχῆς should have been changed to διδαχήν, while the accusative might easily have been changed to the genitive under the influence of the series of adjacent genitives—μετανοίας and πίστεως preceding it and ἐπιθέσεως, ἀναστάσεως, and κρίματος following it.

Moffatt (1924: 73–75) prefers the accusative διδαχήν, although he says "it make no difference which reading is chosen." Zuntz (1953: 93–94) argues strongly for the accusative: the genitive, he submits, is "inadmissible"—not only is it "stylistically bad" but "it makes it impossible to construe the sentence." The committee which produced UBS[3], on the other hand, regarded διδαχήν as a "stylistic improvement introduced in order to avoid so many genitives" (Metzger 1971: 666). Moffatt and Zuntz are right, though Zuntz overstates his case.

Hebrews 9:11

χριστὸς δὲ παραγενόμενος ἀρχιερεὺς τῶν γενομένων ἀγαθῶν

    γενομένων   𝔓[46] (γεναμένων) B D* 1739 lat[d e] syr[pesh hcl pal] Orig Cyr Chrys *al*

    μελλόντων   ℵ A D[c] K P 33 81 *Byz* lat[vg] syr[hcl.mg] cop arm eth Euseb Eph

The evidence is fairly evenly divided between the two readings. Although μελλόντων has majority support, γενομένων has in its favor "the combination of the oldest Greek and Latin with the Syriac evidence," which, says Zuntz, "is in itself almost irresistible" (1953: 119).

Is Christ "high priest of the good things that are to come" or "high priest of the good things that have come to pass"? Either reading makes sense in the context. But since the law is described in Heb 10:1 as having "a shadow of the good things that are to come [τῶν μελλόντων ἀγαθῶν]" it seems probable that the wording of that passage, about which there is no doubt, has influenced the text of Heb 9:11. The "good things that are to come," which were foreshadowed in the law, are now, since the advent of Christ, the "good things that have come to pass."

Hebrews 9:19

λαβὼν τὸ αἷμα τῶν μόσχων [καὶ τῶν τράγων] . . . ἐράντισεν
    τῶν μόσχων καὶ τῶν τράγων   ℵ* A C 81 326 629 2464 *al* lat
      cop^sah.codd
    τῶν μόσχων καὶ τράγων   *Byz* cop^boh
    τῶν τράγων καὶ τῶν μόσχων   D 365 cop^sah.codd
    τῶν μόσχων   𝔓^46 ℵ² K L Ψ 181 1241 1739 1881 2495 *al* syr^pesh
    Orig

For this act of sprinkling did Moses take the blood of calves and goats
or the blood of calves only? The occasion referred to is the institution
of the Sinai covenant, recorded in Exod 24:3–8. The young men who
assisted Moses sacrificed calves (LXX μοσχάρια) as a "peace offering"
to Yahweh (Exod 24:5); it was the blood of these calves that Moses
took and sprinkled. Conformity to the LXX wording (which in this respect follows the MT) would suggest that the shorter text, mentioning
one kind of animal only, is to be preferred. In that case καὶ [τῶν]
τράγων would be an addition made under the influence of Heb 9:12,
where "the blood of goats and calves" is mentioned. (It is certainly the
influence of Heb 9:12 that is responsible for the variant sequence τῶν
τράγων καὶ τῶν μόσχων found in a few witnesses in v. 19.) Zuntz (1953:
55) thinks that the agreement of 𝔓^46 with many later witnesses is a decisive argument for the shorter reading. On the other hand, the
agreement of Alexandrian, "Western," and Byzantine witnesses in favor of the longer reading is impressive. If the longer reading is original, the shorter reading is easily explained by harmonization with
the LXX. UBS¹ originally opted for the shorter reading, but the committee responsible for UBS³ decided to add the words καὶ τῶν τράγων,
but within square brackets, "in order to indicate a certain doubt that
they belong there" (Metzger 1971: 669). The issue remains unde-
cided; on balance (*me iudice*) there is a slight preponderance in favor
of the shorter reading.

Hebrews 10:1

σκιὰν γὰρ ἔχων ὁ νόμος τῶν μελλόντων ἀγαθῶν, οὐκ αὐτὴν τὴν εἰκόνα
τῶν πραγμάτων
    οὐκ αὐτὴν] καί   𝔓^46

The problem here (if problem there be) is not the ascertaining of
the original text, which is not in doubt; it lies in the explanation of

the singular reading καὶ τὴν εἰκόνα instead of οὐκ αὐτὴν τὴν εἰκόνα in 𝔓⁴⁶. (There are a couple of minor variants—οὐ κατά in 69 and οὐκ αὐτῶν in 1908—but these are patent misreadings of οὐκ αὐτήν and need not detain us.) The true text makes a distinction in sense between σκιά and εἰκών—σκιά is a shadow and nothing more, no substitute for the substance, while εἰκών is a replica, if not the equivalent, of the reality itself. Zuntz (1953: 22) compares Iamblichus, *De communi mathematica scientia* 6, which advocates a "turning from the shadows to the images and the light": μεταστροφὴ ἀπὸ τῶν σκιῶν ἐπὶ τὰ εἴδωλα καὶ τὸ φῶς (εἴδωλον being a synonym of εἰκών). Kittel (1964: 393) refers to the legend of Rabbi Banaᵓah (Babylonian Talmud *Baba Batra* 58a), who was permitted to inspect Abraham's tomb, but not Adam's, because (said God) Abraham was made in "the likeness of my image" [*bidĕmût dĕ ᵓîqônî*]" but Adam in "my image itself" [*bidĕyôqānî ᶜaṣmâ*]," Hebrew *ᵓîqôn*, or its reverential transformation *deyôqān*, being a loanword from εἰκών. Adam, according to Gen 1:26–27, was made "in the image [κατ' εἰκόνα] of God," and when Paul speaks of Christ as "the image [εἰκών] of God" (2 Cor 4:4), the implication probably is that he is the "image" of God after which Adam was created. Certainly the description of Christ as the image of God does not suggest that he is but a pale reflection of God; rather, he is the invisible God made visible (cf. Col 1:15).

The reading of 𝔓⁴⁶ is not an accidental misreading: it is a deliberate change of the text rising from a conviction that "image" and "shadow" are practically synonymous, both being set in contrast with the substance or reality. Clement of Alexandria (*Stromata* 6:7:58:770) evidently shared this view: ὁ νόμος σκιὰ καὶ εἰκὼν τῆς ἀληθείας 'the law is a shadow and image of the reality', in fairly clear allusion to Heb 10:1. But it is not the view of the writer to the Hebrews.

Hebrews 10:38

ὁ δὲ δίκαιός μου ἐκ πίστεως ζήσεται
    The above reading is supported by 𝔓⁴⁶ ℵ H* 1739 *al* latᵛᵉᵗ·ᵖˡ vg copˢᵃʰ arm Clem.Alex Theodoret
    ὁ δὲ δίκαιος ἐκ πίστεώς μου ζήσεται   D* 1518 1611 latᵈ ᵉ syrᵖᵉˢʰ ʰᶜˡ Euseb
    ὁ δὲ δίκαιος ἐκ πίστεως ζήσεται   𝔓¹³ Dᶜ Hᶜ K P Ψ *Byz* TR syrᵖᵃˡ copᵇᵒʰ eth Chrys Euthal

This is a quotation from Hab 2:4b (LXX), which adds the possessive μου (not found in the MT). The reading of Heb 10:38 without μου, early and well attested as it is ($\mathfrak{P}^{13}$ belongs to the 3d or 4th century), may safely be left out of the reckoning: it represents most probably an assimilation to the two Pauline instances of the quotation (Gal 3:11, Rom 1:17). The variation in the position of μου is a feature of the LXX text as well as of Heb 10:38. LXX^B reads μου after ἐκ πίστεως, LXX^A reads μου before ἐκ πίστεως (although Codex A itself reads μου in both positions in Hab 2:4b—manifestly a secondary development). While ἐκ πίστεώς μου must mean 'by my faith' (possibly with the force 'by faith in me') or 'by my faithfulness', μου ἐκ πίστεως may have the same sense with greater emphasis on μου or μου may be attached to ὁ δίκαιος 'my righteous one'. It seems likely that μου in the LXX arises from reading Hebrew *ʾĕmûnātô* 'his faith(fulness)', as *ʾĕmûnātî* 'my faith(fulness)'. Most LXX editors regard ἐκ πίστεώς μου as the original text; some indeed regard μου ἐκ πίστεως in the A group as an assimilation of the LXX text to that of Heb 10:38. Most NT editors and exegetes opt for ὁ δὲ δίκαιός μου ἐκ πίστεως ζήσεται in Heb 10:38 (see Zuntz 1953: 173; Metzger 1971: 670–71). T. W. Manson (1945: 124) argues for this as the true LXX reading also: "my righteous one" is the person of God's choice, the Messiah, in other words—the one who will not only live by faithfulness but also "will surely come and not delay." In the context of Heb 10:38, however, each of the readers may qualify as God's "righteous one" and confirm this qualification by pressing on to salvation instead of drawing back to perdition.

Hebrews 11:11

πίστει—καὶ αὐτὴ Σάρρα στεῖρα—δύναμιν εἰς καταβολὴν σπέρματος ἔλαβεν καὶ παρὰ καιρὸν ἡλικίας

    αὐτὴ Σάρρα στεῖρα $\mathfrak{P}^{46}$ D* Ψ lat *om* στειρα $\mathfrak{P}^{13}$ vid ℵ A D^c 33 614
        Byz
    αὐτὴ Σάρρα ἡ στεῖρα   D^1 6 81 1241 1739 1881 *pc*
    αὐτὴ Σάρρα στεῖρα οὖσα   P 104 365 2495 *pc*
    ἔλαβεν] ἔλαβεν εἰς τὸ τεκνῶσαι   D* $\mathfrak{P}$ 81 2495 *pc* lat^b vg.cod
        (syr^{hcl})
    ἡλικίας] ἡλικίας ἔτεκεν   ℵ^2 D^2 *Byz* lat^b syr

The textual question here is bound up with the exegesis of the sentence. Whose faith, according to the author, led to Sarah's pregnancy? The nominative αὐτὴ Σάρρα might suggest that it was Sarah's; the phrase εἰς καταβολὴν σπέρματος shows that it was Abraham's. For καταβολὴ σπέρματος 'the deposition of seed' refers to the father's role in the act of generation. It does not matter how often εἰς καταβολὴν σπέρματος is translated 'for the conception of seed' as though it referred to the mother's role; that is not what καταβολή means.

Tasker (1955: 183) asks if we "know enough about Greek usage at the time to say definitely that an active noun of this kind could not also carry a passive sense"; he mentions the reference in Moulton and Milligan (1930: 324) to a first-century papyrus attestation of καταβολαῖος in the sense of 'store-place'—but καταβολαῖος (sc. τόπος) used thus is "a place where one deposits [καταβάλλει] things." All that we know of the usage of καταβολή makes it most improbable that it could be employed in the sense of conception. "For the conception of seed" would be expressed by εἰς σύλληψιν σπέρματος, and that is not what the author says. A writer so sensitive to Hellenistic usage knew what he intended to say, and knew how to say it.

The situation, however, is complicated on the one hand by the fact that στεῖρα is omitted in the majority of texts, and on the other hand that ἔτεκεν is added after ἡλικίας by the majority text (to the same effect a few other witnesses insert εἰς τὸ τεκνῶσαι before καὶ παρὰ καιρὸν ἡλικίας). If ἔτεκεν 'she gave birth' or εἰς τὸ τεκνῶσαι 'with a view to bearing a child' were original, then Sarah would have perforce to be the subject of the clause, but both additions are based on the assumption that this is so, and represent attempts to make this sense more explicit; they are what Zuntz (1953: 170) calls *Schlimmbesserungen* (false improvements). Without these additions Abraham is as clearly the subject of v. 11 as of vv. 10 and 12: "By faith also he received strength for the deposition of seed when he was past the age for it."

But what of Sarah, who receives honorable mention in the text as it stands? If στεῖρα be accepted, then καὶ αὐτὴ Σάρρα στεῖρα is best treated, as in UBS[3], as a circumstantial clause: "Sarah herself being barren" (cf. Black 1967: 83–89). If στεῖρα, on the other hand, is no part of the original text, then αὐτὴ Σάρρα is best construed in the dative (αὐτῇ Σάρρᾳ), the dative of accompaniment: "By faith also, together with Sarah, he received strength . . . " (cf. Riggenbach 1922: 356ff.; Michel 1949: 262).

More drastic is the attempt to reject αὐτὴ Σάρρα from the text as a gloss (Field 1899: 232; Windisch 1931: 101; Zuntz 1953: 16): "καὶ αὐτή makes a poor connexion (it is typical of 'Scholiasten Griechisch'): 'likewise' is the only admissible translation. This makes nonsense of the context: who else is said to have received, through faith, δύναμιν εἰς καταβολὴν σπέρματος?" These objections of Zuntz to the genuineness of αὐτὴ Σάρρα are met if we are dealing here with a circumstantial clause (καὶ αὐτὴ Σάρρα στεῖρα) or with a dative of accompaniment (αὐτῇ Σάρρᾳ).

Hebrews 11:37

ἐλιθάσθησαν, ἐπρίσθησαν, ἐν φόνῳ μαχαίρης ἀπέθανον
> ἐλιθάσθησαν ἐπρίσθησαν $\mathfrak{P}^{46}$ 1241 1981 *pc* syr^pesh eth^ro pp
> Orig^gr 2/7, lat Euseb Eph Hier *al*
> ἐπρίσθησαν ἐλιθάσθησαν cop^sah
> ἐλιθάσθησαν ἐπειράσθησαν lat^vg.cod Clem.Alex
> ἐλιθάσθησαν ἐπιράσθησαν ἐπιράσθησαν D*
> ἐλιθάσθησαν ἐπρίσθησαν ἐπειράσθησαν $\mathfrak{P}^{13 vid}$ A D² K 88 *Byz* lat^vet vg
> (syr^pal) cop^boh arm Orig Eph Ambr Chrys Theodoret Joh.Dam
> ἐλιθάσθησαν ἐπρήσθησαν ἐπειράσθησαν Ψ^vid 1923
> ἐλιθάσθησαν ἐπειράσθησαν ἐπρίσθησαν ℵ L P 048 (ἐπιρ- for ἐπειρ-)
> 33 81 326 2495 *pc* syr^pesh hcl cop^boh.cod Euthal

The sequence in $\mathfrak{P}^{46}$ and other witnesses, "they were stoned, they were sawn in two, they were killed with the sword (beheaded)," lists various kinds of capital punishment (stoning, as in 2 Chr 24:21, and beheading, as in Jer 26:23, are attested in the OT, while the sawing in two is perhaps a reference to the legend of Isaiah's martyrdom). The insertion of ἐπειράσθησαν 'they were exposed to trial' in this list is unnatural. A comparative examination of the witnesses suggests strongly that ἐπρίσθησαν without ἐπειράσθησαν is the original reading, ἐπειράσθησαν being a "corrupt dittography" (Zuntz 1953: 47). So already Erasmus and Calvin.

The fact that ἐπειράσθησαν appears in several witnesses before and not after ἐπρίσθησαν is a further indication of its secondary character. The form ἐπιράσθησαν (curiously duplicated) in D* is an itacistic spelling of ἐπειράσθησαν. The reading of Ψ^vid and 1923, ἐπρήσθησαν, is an itacistic spelling of ἐπρίσθησαν, but as spelled it happens to make good sense ('they were burnt'). Various attempts to emend ἐπειράσθησαν to a form deemed more appropriate in the context (for a list see Metzger 1971: 674) have been as unsuccessful as they are unnecessary.

Hebrews 12:1

ὄγκον ἀποθέμενοι πάντα καὶ τὴν εὐπερίστατον ἁμαρτίαν
> εὐπερίστατον $\mathfrak{P}^{13}$ ℵ A D K P Ψ *Byz* lat syr cop cett
> εὐπερίσπαστον $\mathfrak{P}^{46}$ 1739

The attestation of εὐπερίστατον 'easily entangling' is so preponderant that the only reason for giving serious consideration to the variant εὐπερίσπαστον 'easily distracting' is its appearance in the oldest extant witness (𝔓⁴⁶). For the sense of εὐπερίσπαστος we may compare ἀπερισπάστως 'without distraction' in 1 Cor 7:35. Zuntz (1953: 25–29) argues in favor of εὐπερίσπαστον in Heb 12:1: "the meanings which can be attached to the rival reading [εὐπερίστατον] are so far inferior to this," he says, "as to make it justifiable, nay necessary, to regard the reading of 𝔓⁴⁶ as original." He adds that εὐπερίστατον could only mean "'surrounded by many', primarily in admiration." But the aptness of εὐπερίστατον to the context is defended by Simpson (1946: 26–27): he notes the converse term ἀπερίστατος 'unencumbered' used of Diogenes by Epictetus (*Dissertationes* 4:1:159) and suggests "sin *so prone to hamper* or *trammel*" as the sense of Heb 12:1. According to Metzger (1971: 675), "εὐπερίσπαστον is either a paleographical error or a deliberate modification of εὐπερίστατον."

Hebrews 12:3

ἀναλογίσασθε γὰρ τὸν τοιαύτην ὑπομεμενηκότα ὑπὸ τῶν ἁμαρτωλῶν εἰς ἑαυτὸν ἀντιλογίαν

    εἰς ἑαυτόν/εἰς αὐτόν   A Dᶜ K P Ψ* 88 104 181 326 614 1241
       1739ᶜ 1877 1881 2495 Chrys Joh.Dam
    εἰς ἑαυτούς/εἰς αὐτούς   𝔓¹³ 𝔓⁴⁶ ℵ*ᵇ D* Ψ² 048 33 81 451 1739*
       2127 2492 Orig Eph *al*

The plural pronoun has earliest and strongest attestation. But what is the sense in this context of "the opposition of sinners against them(selves)"? It is pointless to draw attention to Num 16:38 (17:3 MT, LXX), "sinners against themselves" (τῶν ἁμαρτωλῶν τούτων ἐν ταῖς ψυχαῖς αὐτῶν), as do Westcott and Hort (1881: 612): apart from anything else, the construction of Heb 12:3 would require εἰς ἑαυτούς (if that were the reading) to be taken with ἀντιλογίαν, not with ἁμαρτωλῶν. Attempts to make sense of the plural, like those of Inge (1933: 14)—"He, whom we so often 'contradict,' is our true self"—are unsuccessful. Riggenbach (1922: 391) does not exaggerate in saying that the plural reading is "very strongly attested, but absolutely meaningless." Zuntz (1953: 120) rightly discerns in the plural reading "one more instance of that 'primitive corruption' which Westcott and Hort [1882: 129] recognized in this epistle," a corruption which was corrected by a happy conjecture which must approximate closely to the original text.

* * *

An amateur in textual criticism might well feel some trepidation in offering an exercise like this to Dr. Greenlee. His pioneer work on Codex Zacynthius and the gospel text of Cyril of Jerusalem, together with his *Introduction to New Testament Textual Criticism* have long since vindicated his standing as an authority in the text-critical field. An exegete welcomes the textual critic's aid in establishing a reliable text as an indispensable prerequisite for his own studies. If one conclusion emerges from the examination of these textual problems in Hebrews, it is the inevitable interrelation between text and exegesis, with the corollary that textual criticism must always be "rational"—must always do justice to the sense intended by the author. In friendship and admiration, then, I gladly make this contribution to the volume in honor of Dr. Greenlee.

References

Anderson, C. P.
   1966   "The Epistle to the Hebrews and the Pauline Letter Collection."
           Harvard Theological Review 59:429–38.
Bengel, J. A.
   1734   *Gnomon Novi Testamenti.* London: Williams & Norgate, 1862.
Black, Matthew
   1967   *An Aramaic Approach to the Gospels and Acts.* 3d edition. Oxford:
           Clarendon.
Field, Frederick
   1899   *Notes on the Translation of the New Testament.* Cambridge: Cam-
           bridge University Press.
von Harnack, Adolf
   1929   *Zwei alte dogmatische Korrekturen im Hebräerbrief.* Sitzungsberichte
           der preussischen Akademie der Wissenschaften, phil.-hist.
           Klasse.
Inge, William Ralph
   1933   *Things New and Old.* London: Longmans Green.
Kittel, Gerhard
   1964   "εἰκών." Vol. 2: pp. 381–97 in *Theological Dictionary of the New Tes-
           tament.* Edited by Gerhard Kittel and Gerhard Friedrich. Grand
           Rapids: Eerdmans.
Manson, T. W.
   1945   "The Argument from Prophecy." *Journal of Theological Studies*
           46:129–36.

Manson, William
1951   *The Epistle to the Hebrews.* Baird Lecture. London: Hodder & Stoughton.
Metzger, Bruce Manning
1971   *A Textual Commentary on the Greek New Testament.* London/New York: United Bible Societies.
Michel, Otto
1949   *Der Brief an die Hebräer.* Kritisch-exegetischer Kommentar über das Neue Testament. Göttingen: Vandenhoeck & Ruprecht.
Moffatt, James
1924   *A Critical and Exegetical Commentary on the Epistle to the Hebrews.* International Critical Commentary. Edinburgh: T. & T. Clark.
Moulton, James Hope, and George Milligan
1930   *The Vocabulary of the Greek Testament.* London: Hodder & Stoughton.
Riggenbach, E.
1922   *Der Brief an die Hebräer.* Leipzig: Deichert.
Simpson, Edmund K.
1946   *Words Worth Weighing in the Greek New Testament.* London: Tyndale.
Tasker, R. V. G.
1955   "The Text of the 'Corpus Paulinum.'" *New Testament Studies* 1:182–91.
Westcott, B. F., and F. J. A. Hort
1881   *The New Testament in the Original Greek.* Volume 1: *Text.* London: Macmillan.
1882   *The New Testament in the Original Greek.* Volume 2: *Introduction, Appendix.* London: Macmillan.
Windisch, Hans
1931   *Der Hebräerbrief.* Handbuch zum Neuen Testament. Tübingen: Mohr.
Zuntz, Günther
1953   *The Text of the Epistles.* Schweich Lectures 1946. London: Oxford University Press for the British Academy.

New Testament Linguistic Usage

J. K. Elliott
University of Leeds

Each of the NT authors has his own characteristic style and usage in matters of grammar, vocabulary, and word order. Attempts have been made in recent years, not only in grammars of NT Greek but also in numerous articles and monographs, to isolate and describe some of the distinctive features of several of the writings in the canon. These but seldom take into account the critical apparatus to the printed testament. All too often decisions are reached, rules of usage cataloged, and apparent exceptions to these "rules" noted without taking textual variation into the picture.

The following short studies try to isolate three features of NT usage—the position of ἐκεῖνος in the Gospels and Acts, the position of the dative of αὐτός in John, and the expression πρός με/ἐμέ in the NT as a whole. These three serve as examples to show how the use of concordance and text alone—essential though these are in the description of grammatical features in the NT—needs to be supplemented by the evidence of the manuscripts.

For such study I acknowledge the pioneering work of C. H. Turner, who in the 1920s contributed a series of articles to the *Journal of Theological Studies* on Markan usage. I also acknowledge the

42   J. K. Elliott

work of G. D. Kilpatrick, who followed in Turner's footsteps, and
with whom I discussed many aspects of NT style, including the three
topics below.

Dr. Greenlee's painstaking work on NT manuscripts and his
splendid achievements in popularizing the discipline of textual criticism are deservedly well known. It is indeed a great honour and
pleasure to be associated with this volume of essays.

ἐκεῖνος in the Gospels and Acts

Matthew

1. pronominal (total: 4 + 2):
   13:11; 17:27; 20:4; 24:43; κἀκεῖνος is always pronominal: 15:18;
   23:23
2. adjectival:
   a. follows its noun (total: 34 + 8 *v.l.*):[1]
      3:1 *v.l.*; 7:25, 27; 8:13, 28; 9:22, 26, 31; 10:14, 15; 12:45; 13:1,
      44; 14:35a *v.l.*, 35b; 15:22, 28; 17:18; 18:7 *v.l.*, 26 *v.l.*, 27 *v.l.*,
      28, 32; 21:40; 22:7, 10; 24:22 (*bis*), 29, 36, 38 *v.l.*, 46, 48 *v.l.*, 50;
      25:7, 19; 26:24 (*bis*), 29; 27:8, 19, 63 *v.l.*
   b. precedes its noun:
      (i) ἐν + ἡμέρα   sing. 7:22; 22:23; but cf. 13:1
           ἐν + ἡμέρα   plur. 3:1 *v.l.*; 24:19; cf. 24:38 *v.l.*
           ἐν + καιρός   11:25; 12:1; 14:1
           ἐν + ὥρα   8:13 *v.l.*; 10:19; 18:1; 26:55
      (ii) ἀπὸ + ἡμέρα   22:46, but not ὥρα; cf. 9:22; 15:28; 17:18

Mark

1. except for 7:20 (*q.v.*) the variant ἐκεῖνοι at 4:20 and for κἀκεῖνοι at
   12:4, 5, ἐκεῖνος is not used pronominally; contrast Pseudo-Mark
   16:10, 11, 13 (*bis*), 20, where it is so used
2. demonstrative adjective:
   a. follows its noun (total: 9 + 1 *v.l.*):
      3:24, 25; 6:11 *v.l.*, 55; 13:19, 24b, 32; 14:21 (*bis*), 25
   b. precedes its noun:
      (i) (total: 7):

---

1. As the 8 variants include the demonstrative in a position compatible with
Matthew's practice in the 34 firm examples, a strong case could be made for accepting as original those variant readings adding the demonstrative, but note that under
#2b different conditions may apply at 3:1 or 24:38 in a set phrase following ἐν. In the
case of 27:63 the sequence article + noun + demonstrative is to be preferred.

ἐν + ἡμέρα sing. 2:20; 4:35
ἐν + ἡμέρα plur. 1:9; 8:1; 13:17, 24a
ἐν + ὥρα sing. 13:11

(ii) 4:11 ἐκείνοις δὲ τοῖς ἔξω (the alternative would be τοῖς δὲ ἔξω ἐκείνοις)

(iii) 12:7 ἐκεῖνοι δὲ οἱ γεωργοί (but D lat read οἱ δὲ γεωργοί, a reading that may be original)

Luke

1. pronominal (total: 2 [+3 *v.l.*] + 4):[2]
   8:32; 9:34 *v.l*; 12:38 *v.l*; 18:14 *v.l*; 19:4; κἀκεῖνος is always pronominal: 11:7, 42; 20:11; 22:12

2. adjectival:
   a. follows its noun (total: 19 + 3 *v.l.*)
      2:1; 4:2; 6:48, 49; 9:5; 10:12b, 31; 11:26; 12:37, 43, 45, 46; 14:21 *v.l.*,[3] 24; 15:14, 15; 17:9 *v.l*; 18:3; 20:1 *v.l*, 35; 21:34; 22:22
   b. precedes its noun:
      (i)   ἐν + ἡμέρα   sing. 6:23; 17:31
            ἐν + ἡμέρα   plur. 5:35; 9:36; 21:23
            ἐν + ὥρα   7:21
            (N.B. ἐκεῖνος *after* ἡμέρα in the phrases ἐν τῇ ἡμέρᾳ ἐκείνῃ in 10:12a and ἐν ταῖς ἡμέραις ἐκείναις in 2:1; 4:2)
      (ii) others: 12:47; 13:4; 20:18

Acts

1. pronominal:
   3:13; 10:9 *v.l*, 10 *v.l*; 21:6; κἀκεῖνος is always pronominal: 5:37; 15:11; 18:19

2. adjectival:
   a. follows its noun (total: 15 + 1 *v.l.*):
      1:19; 2:18 (LXX; the *v.l.* omits ἐκεῖνος), 41; 3:23 (OT quotation); 7:41; 8:8; 9:37; 12:6; 14:21; 16:3, 35; 19:16, 23; 20:2; 22:11; 28:7
   b. precedes its noun:
      (i)   ἐν + ἡμέρα   sing. 8:1 (ἐκεῖνος follows ἡμέρα in 2:41)
            ἐν + ἡμέρα   plur. (no occurrences, but ἐκεῖνος follows ἡμέρα in 2:18 *v.l*; 7:41; 9:37)

2. Again, the problem of the variants may be resolved by a comparison with the firm examples. At 18:14 the longer reading by D is not consistent with #2a below.

3. An original ἐκεῖνος could easily have been omitted accidentally through homoioteleuton; the same is true of ἐκείνῳ at 17:9 and ἐκεινῶν at 20:1.

ἐν + ὥρα 16:33

(ii) κατὰ + καιρός 12:1 (ἐκεῖνος follows καιρός in 19:23)

John

1. pronominal:
   a. before the verb (total: 26 + 2 *v.l.*):
      2:21; 3:30; 5:19, 35, 37, 39, 43, 46, 47; 8:42, 44; 9:9, 28 *v.l.*, 37;
      10:1, 6, 35; 11:13, 29; 12:48; 13:26; 14:21, 26; 15:26; 16:14;
      19:21, 35 (*v.l.* κἀκεῖνος); 20:15
      κἀκεῖνος always before the verb (total: 5 + 1 *v.l.*): 6:57; 7:29;
      10:16; 14:12; 17:24; 19:35 (*v.l.* ἐκεῖνος)
   b. after the verb (total: 19 + 5 *v.l.*):
      1:8; 3:28; 4:25; 5:38; 6:22 *v.l.*, 29; 7:11, 45; 9:11, 12, 25, 28 *v.l.*,
      36 *v.l.*; 13:6 *v.l.*, 25, 27, 30; 16:8, 13; 18:17, 25; 19:15 *v.l.*; 20:13,
      16
2. adjectival:
   a. follows its noun (total: 12 + 1 *v.l.*):
      1:18(?), 33, 39; 4:39; 5:11; 11:49, 51; 18:13, 15; 19:31 *v.l.*;[4]
      20:19, 21:7, 23
   b. precedes its noun (total: 8):
      (i)   ἐν + ἡμέρα   5:9; 14:20; 16:23, 26
            ἐν + ὥρα   4:53
            ἐν + νύξ   21:3
      (ii) ἀπὸ + ἡμέρα   11:53
            ἀπὸ + ὥρα   19:27
      (iii) in 7 out of 8 instances where ἐκεῖνος precedes its noun,
            not merely does the demonstrative precede its noun but
            the whole phrase precedes the verb; the exception is 5:9:
            ἦν δὲ σάββατον ἐν ἐκείνη τῇ ἡμέρα, where ἐν ἐκείνη τῇ
            ἡμέρᾳ is omitted by D, which would give a sentence like
            13:30: ἦν δὲ νύξ or 18:28 ἦν δὲ πρωί; the strangeness of
            the longer text inclines me to favor the reading of D
            here (the presence of οὖν prevents resolving the prob-
            lem by repunctuating: Ἦν δέ σάββατον. ἐν ἐκείνη τῇ
            ἡμέρα ἔλεγον . . .)

---

4. This is a particularly interesting variant, being a choice between ἡ ἡμέρα
ἐκείνου τοῦ σαββάτου and ἡ ἡμέρα ἐκείνη τοῦ σαββάτου. Johannine usage here suggests
the latter is likely to be original even (or especially) with ἡμέρα (cf. 1:39, 20:19).

Conclusions

1. pronominal:
   a. κἀκεῖνος is always pronominal
   b. the authors differ concerning pronominal ἐκεῖνος, which is apparently unknown in Mark but common in John, where (against the dominant practice) it precedes the verb more often than not; it occurs in Matthew, Luke, Acts, but not as often as in John
2. adjectival:
   a. adjectival ἐκεῖνος as a rule follows its noun
   b. the exceptions are similar; ἐκεῖνος precedes the noun in the following phrases:

Mark:	ἐν + ἡμέρα (sing. and plur.) and ἐν + ὥρα
John:	ἐν + ἡμέρα (sing.), ἐν + ὥρα, ἐν + νύξ, ἀπὸ + ἡμέρα, and ἀπὸ + ὥρα
Luke:	ἐν + ἡμέρα (sing. and plur.) and four other phrases
Matthew:	ἐν + ἡμέρα (sing. and plur.), ἐν + καιρός, ἐν + ὥρα, ἀπό + ἡμέρα
Acts:	ἐν + ἡμέρα (sing.), ἐν + ὥρα, and κατὰ + καιρός

Position of αὐτῷ, αὐτῇ, and αὐτοῖς in John, When the Pronoun Does Not Depend on a Preposition

αὐτῷ

1. usually immediately after the verb:
   1:22 (οὖν+), 25, 39, 40, 41, 42, 43, 45, 46 (*bis*), 48 (*bis*), 49, 50, 51; 2:10, 18; 3:2, 3, 9, 10, 26, 27; 4:9 (οὖν+), 11, 14 (*bis*), 17, 19, 25, 33, 50 (*bis*), 51, 52, 53; 5:6, 7, 8, 14, 20, 27; 6:2, 7, 8, 25, 30 (οὖν+), 65, 68; 7:52; 8:13 (οὖν+), 19 (οὖν+), 25 (οὖν+), 29, 31, 33, 39, 41 (οὖν+), 48, 52 (οὖν+); 9:7, 10 (οὖν+), 26 (δὲ+), 34, 35, 37 (*v.l.* δὲ +), 38, 40; 10:13, 24, 33; 11:8, 12, 20, 24, 27, 30, 32, 34, 39; 12:2 (οὖν+), 6, 16, 18, 34; 13:3, 6, 7, 8 (*bis*), 9, 10, 24, 25, 26, 27 (οὖν+), 28, 29, 36 (*bis*), 37, 38; 14:5, 6, 8, 9, 21, 22, 23; 16:29; 17:2 (*bis.*); 18:5, 20, 23, 25 (οὖν+), 30, 31, (οὖν+), 33, 34, 37 (οὖν+), 38; 19:3, 7, 9, 10 (οὖν+), 11, 32; 20:6, 15, 16, 25 (οὖν+), 28, 29; 21:3, 5, 15 (*bis*), 16 (*bis*), 17 (4x), 19, 22, 23
2. after other words:
   1:6; 3:1; 8:29; 9:9; 12:13
3. before the verb:
   7:26; 10:4; 12:29

αὐτῇ

always immediately after the verb:
   2:4; 4:7, 10, 13, 16, 17, 21, 26; 11:23, 25, 31, 33, 40; 20:13, 15, 16,
   17, 18

αὐτοῖς

always immediately after the verb:
   1:12, 26, 38, 39; 2:7, 8, 19, 24 (ἑαυτὸν+); 4:32, 34; 5:11, 17, 19; 6:7,
   20, 26, 29, 31, 32 (οὖν+), 35 (δὲ+), 43, 53 (οὖν+), 61, 70; 7:6 (οὖν+),
   9, 16, 21, 45, 47 (οὖν+); 8:12 v.l., 14, 21 (οὖν πάλιν+), 21, 23, 25, 28
   (οὖν+), 34, 39, 42, 58; 9:15, 20, 27, 30, 41; 10:6 (bis), 7 (οὖν πά-
   λιν+), 25, 28, 32, 34; 11:11, 14, 44, 46, 49; 12:23, 35 (οὖν+); 13:12;
   15:22; 16:19, 31; 17:2, 8, 14, 22, 26; 18:4, 5, 6, 21, 31 (οὖν+), 38;
   19:4, 5, 6, 15, 16 (αὐτόν+); 20:2, 13, 17, 19, 20, 21 (οὖν+), 22 v.l.,
   22, 23, 25; 21:3, 5 (οὖν+), 6, 10, 12, 13

Principles governing position

In the main all forms occupy the same position in the sentence.
They come immediately after the verb or other word on which they
depend. Οὖν intervenes between them and the verb some 27 times,
δέ perhaps thrice. At this point agreement ceases. Αὐτῷ comes before its verb thrice, αὐτῇ and αὐτοῖς never. On the other hand αὐτῷ
precedes πάλιν at 9:26 and 21:16, but πάλιν precedes αὐτοῖς 8:21 and
10:7. Αὐτῷ precedes ἐμαυτόν at 14:21, but ἑαυτόν precedes αὐτοῖς at
2:24. Αὐτόν precedes αὐτοῖς at 19:16.

   The three instances of αὐτῷ before the verb remain a problem.
At 10:4 αὐτῷ is contrasted with ἀλλοτρίῳ at the beginning of 10:5 and
this may account for the forward position here, but no such explanation is available for 7:26 or 12:29.

Note on the textual evidence

   Words like πάλιν or αὐτῷ are often textually insecure. The variants at the crucial passages are as follows:

2:24	ἑαυτὸν	𝔓⁶⁶ W Θ Ρ Γ Δ Π
	αυτον	ℵ A* B L 700
8:21	αὐτοῖς πάλιν	053 517 713 1424 <u>al</u> <u>a</u> <u>c</u> <u>q</u>
	πάλιν omitted	ℵ 0141
9:26	πάλιν	𝔓⁶⁶ A Θ Χ Γ Δ Λ
	omitted	𝔓⁷⁵ ℵ B D W
10:7	πάλιν αὐτοῖς	ℵ D L M Θ U Γ Δ
	αὐτοῖς πάλιν	A Π Λ Y

πάλιν omitted 𝔓⁴⁵ 𝔓⁶⁶ ℵ W 0141
αὐτοῖς omitted ℵ B
21:16   πάλιν before λέγει ℵ C W Θ
πάλιν omitted D c̲ e̲

The longer text is reasonably firm at 8:21 and 9:26. There is a general tendency for scribes to omit πάλιν and the various forms of αὐτός. This leaves us with the variant at 2:24 and the variations in order at 8:21; 10:7 and 21:16. The evangelist, like other NT writers, uses the uncontracted reflexive ἑαυτόν and not the Attic αὐτὸν, which is probably intended by αυτον at 2:24. Πάλιν αὐτοῖς at 10:7 is compatible with 8:21 (v.l.) and should probably be read here as the original text. Πάλιν λέγει at 21:16 likewise is probably the original reading—altered because of its apparent awkwardness.

πρός με or πρὸς ἐμέ in the New Testament

Blass-Debrunner-Funk §279 states that in oblique cases the accented form of the first-person singular pronoun is used in NT Greek (as in Classical Greek) to denote emphasis and contrast. In the NT, however, there are exceptions after πρός, but the printed editions do not give a consistent picture.

While there is no undoubted example of πρὸς ἐμέ in the NT, the manuscripts are unanimously for πρός με at Matt 3:14, 11:28; Luke 6:47; John 5:40; Acts 22:10, 26:14; and Titus 3:12. At Matt 3:14 πρός με is emphatic, and so we cannot distinguish between πρὸς ἐμέ emphatic and πρός με unemphatic. It is probable that position rather than accentuation provided the means of emphasizing in this phrase. Ἐμέ is supported by the following manuscript evidence in the passages listed:

Matt	19:14	ℵ L Δ
	25:36	ℵ
Mark	9:19	𝔓⁴⁵ ℵ
	10:14	N W
Luke	1:43	ℵ* B Θ
	14:26	𝔓⁴⁵ ℵ
	18:16	W
John	6:35	ℵ B D (deest 𝔓⁶⁶)
	6:37a	all except L Λ Π (ME)
	6:37b	𝔓⁶⁶ ℵ D E K Δ Θ 047 440 1207

	6:44	ℵ D E M U V Δ Θ 047 471 461 2145
	6:45	ℵ B D Θ 1675 Or
	6:65	ℵ C
	7:37	B
Acts	11:11	ℵ* 1765
	22:8	ℵ* A B
	22:13	ℵ* A B
	22:21	C
	23:22	ℵ B 429
	24:19	ℵ A B C E 33 81 337 1175 1739
1 Cor	16:11	$\mathfrak{P}^{46}$ B D F G 823 1175 1912
Phil	2:30	$\mathfrak{P}^{46}$ ℵ
2 Tim	4:9	D

We should probably regard ἐμέ in all these instances as a correction to the grammarians' rules. It is printed in the text of NA[26] at Luke 1:43; John 6:35, 37 (*bis*), 45; and Acts 24:19.

From this evidence it is clear that Alexandrian manuscripts have frequently suffered this kind of correction. On the other hand the so-called Byzantine texts are remarkably free. Only at John 6:37 had ἐμέ penetrated both Byzantine texts and the Textus Receptus.

The Shape of Life in the Spirit in Pauline Thought

David S. Dockery
Southern Baptist Theological Seminary

Introductory Considerations

The history of the interpretation of Pauline thought within Pietistic and Scholastic orthodoxy is one that traditionally has seen Paul primarily as a systematic theologian. There has been a lack of regard for the apostle's own situation or the situation of his audience. Thus, the writings found in the Pauline corpus have been seen as a body of theological literature more or less chiseled in stone. This approach to Paul was challenged with partial success by the historical-critical approach to interpretation of the Tübingen school. This school of thought brought to our attention the historical setting of the NT writings. This was helpful for the Pauline materials and shed much light on the interpretation of the letters. While the results of traditional exegesis found almost total unity in the literature, the Tübingen school concluded that the letters were extremely diverse. It has since become accepted that there is both unity and diversity in the literature. The problem, however, is that those emphasizing diversity, similar to those who maintain consistency and unity, sometimes failed to consider the existence of contextual applicational and/or development in the

Pauline materials. They have, according to R. Longenecker, thereby turned the figure of the apostle into something resembling "the frigid stone statuary of Europe's cathedrals" (1979: 196).

Occasionally, the question of development in Paul has come to the fore in NT studies since Sabatier's attempt in the late nineteenth century (1896) to trace out what he called "the progressive character of Paulinism." It is not my intention to trace the history of this approach to Pauline studies. Sabatier's entrance into this realm was not the initial exploration of Pauline development. M. F. Wiles (1976) has documented the developmental approach to Pauline thought as early as Chrysostom in the Antiochean school among the Ante-Nicene fathers. An annotated bibliography of the advocates of the development approach in Pauline thought has been compiled by J. C. Hurd Jr. (1965: 8–9).

Indications of Pauline Development

Within the apostle's primary writings, there is a continual concern for ongoing maturity in his life and further understanding of God's revelation. Immediately, several passages come to mind that indicate a consciousness of Paul's own growth in matters of mental and moral perfection. In Phil 1:9–11, he writes:

> And this is my prayer: that your love may abound more and more in knowledge and depth of insight, so that you may be able to discern what is best and may be pure and blameless until the day of Christ, filled with the fruit of righteousness that comes through Jesus Christ—to the glory and praise of God.

In Gal 3:24–4:7, we find another example of developmental language. Formerly, before Christ, he referred to Israel under the Law as a child (νήπιος). Now, believers in Christ are no longer children or slaves, but full-grown children, having been adopted (υἱοθεσία), having the full rights of an "heir." There seems to be further reference to such conscious thought of growth and development in 1 Cor 3:1–15. The divisive church members are described as "infants" (νήπιοι) in Christ for whom Paul wishes full maturity (vv. 1–4); then he changes the metaphor representing the church as a field where he planted the seed, Apollos watered it, but God made it grow (vv. 5–9); and lastly he depicts the church as a building for which he laid a foundation upon which others are building (vv. 10–15).

Two impressive statements are found in 1 Cor 13:9–12 and in Phil 3:12–16. In the first, Paul expresses regret that his ultimate development is incomplete. He says:

For we know in part and prophesy in part, but when perfection comes, the imperfect disappears. When I was a child I talked like a child, I thought like a child, I reasoned like a child. When I became a man, I put childish ways behind me. Now we see but a poor reflection; then we shall see face to face. Now I know in part; then I shall know fully, even as I am fully known.

The final example comes from a passage written late in the apostle's career. Yet, he says:

Not that I have already obtained all this, or have already been made perfect, but I press on to take hold of that for which Christ Jesus took hold of me. Brothers, I do not consider myself yet to have taken hold of it. But one thing I do; forgetting what is behind and straining toward what is ahead, I press on toward the goal to win the prize for which God has called me heavenward in Christ Jesus. All of us who are mature should take such a view of things. And if on some point you think differently that too God will make clear to you. Only let us live up to what we have already attained.

Paul's own spiritual development is part of Luke's account of Acts 9:22: "Yet Saul grew more and more powerful. . . ." It will require further evidence from exegesis to show the possibility of development in Pauline thought in his theological affirmations and ethical reflections which parallel his own personal spiritual development. However, it seems that within Paul's own mind there are indications of mental and moral development in his own writings. I concur with Sir William Ramsay in the following observations:

Paul is penetrated from first to last with this idea [development]. He looks at everything as a process of growth, not as a hard stationary given fact. The true life is making towards perfection through growth, culminating in fruit. How frequently there appears in his letters this thought of producing fruit, a development leading towards an issue in rights and usefulness. The good seems never to occur to his mind as a mere quality, but as a law of progress. . . . His whole philosophy rests on this idea of growth and development. The world is always to him fluid and changing, never stationary. But the change is towards an end, not mere flux without law; it is either degeneration towards death or increase towards perfection and true life (Ramsay 1960: 33).

These words serve as an appropriate conclusion for this section. I now focus upon the questions of method.

Methodological Questions

It is not my intention to hide the objections that can be raised in my attempt to trace out Pauline development related to the spiritual life. M. J. Harris has reminded us of several objections that form "easily discernible signposts which remind travellers of the hazards of the way" (1971: 33). Longenecker has aptly summarized these warning signs (1979: 199).

First, there is the obvious question relating to the extent of the Pauline corpus itself, which is not a mitigating factor for seven of the letters, but does pose questions for Ephesians, Colossians, 2 Thessalonians, and the Pastoral Epistles. Then, of course, there are problems having to do with the chronological sequence of and historical relations between, not only the letters themselves, but also in some cases, material within the present form of the letters. In addition, all of the extant letters fall within a relatively brief fifteen-year period of the apostle's life when some might suppose a certain level of maturity had been reached in his thought.[1] J. C. Beker has carefully analyzed the circumstantial and contextual nature of the writings. His monumental work, *Paul the Apostle* (1980), is a description of the pastoral and polemical nature of much that Paul says in his letters, which demands a contextual rather than a systematic treatment of the subject matter. If we take seriously the contextual nature of the letters, then certain arguments from silence, which have been frequently employed in support of various developmental theories, are notoriously insecure. We should not forget the presence of tension within Christian truth. This in itself makes it exceedingly difficult to classify Paul's theology, either in its parts or its entirety, according to any developmental stages. As we progress in the outworkings of this essay, we must keep in mind these warnings.

The Meaning of Development in Pauline Literature

If it can be granted that there is some element of development in Pauline thought, the question remains, What is meant by development in general and by development in Pauline thought particularly? Is the development from the simple to the complex, from the basic to the advanced, following traditional biological thought? It seems important to distinguish between the idea of development

1. Ryrie (1959: 164) says, "We may notice change of emphases in his epistles, but not change of doctrine . . . , therefore his theology was fully developed from the first stroke of his pen."

and evolution. C. F. D. Moule, in *The Origin of Christology* (1979), has helped make this distinction. I am not suggesting a Darwinian pattern in Pauline thought. Other questions must be considered: Is it possible that the development does not necessarily advance? Does the development have continuity? If it does have some degree of continuity (often expressed as unity and variety), what is the central thought within the continuity?[2]

It is nearly impossible to discover someone who does not acknowledge some form of development in Christian theology over the past two thousand years. Likewise, there is an acknowledged development within the canon itself, whether referred to as "advancement in religion" (with the emphasis upon the evolving human thought), or "theological development" (emphasis upon both the human and divine), or "progressive revelation" (with the emphasis primarily upon the divine). Yet there is little, if any, agreement regarding development within a single author.[3]

The question for my purposes relates to what is meant by development in Paul's writings. Can we offer a model or combination of models that will accurately account for the unity and variety in the Pauline materials? Following my examination of the texts in the next portion of the essay, we will be able to interact with those important questions.

Exegetical Considerations

My purpose in this section is to examine and summarize the primary Pauline texts relating to the spiritual life. An attempt to deal with Paul's view of Spirit in the traditional fashion of systematic theologians as an aspect of the Christian Trinity world be inappropriate for my purposes. This is certainly not to deny that the Spirit is for Paul a distinct entity over against the Father and Son; nor is it meant to contradict later ontological statements concerning the Holy

2. Much traditional interpretation of Pauline thought has followed Martin Luther's proposal that "justification by faith" is the core of Pauline thought. Beker (1980) suggests the theme of "apocalyptic triumph." Richard Gaffin's 1978 proposal is quite similar. F. F. Bruce (1977) and R. N. Longenecker (1964 and 1975) offer the idea of freedom as the characteristic theme of Paul's thought. Ralph P. Martin (1981) opts for the theme of reconciliation.

3. If there is development of thought within each author, it could conceivably have an impact upon decisions regarding authorial authenticity, although issues of authorship have given way in many areas to newer interests such as literary questions (cf. Martin 1981: 157; Sanders 1984: 1–20).

Spirit. But the viewpoint of Paul is primarily that of a concern with redemptive history.[4]

The passages which I shall discuss are viewed within their larger contexts, not as selected verses chosen on the basis of their importance for my thought and purposes. These passages will be examined in what has traditionally been considered the chronological order of the letters. I would also like to note the possibility of an important experience in Paul's life prior to the time when his extant letters were written. This spiritual encounter is mentioned in 2 Cor 12:1–10. In addition, I shall note briefly Paul's rabbinic background before devoting my primary focus to Gal 5:13–16, 1 Cor 12:14, 2 Cor 3:7–18, 2 Cor 12:1–10, and Romans 7–8.

Background Considerations

Spirit in Rabbinic Judaism. The background of Paul's thought is best located in Palestinian Judaism. This interpretation wishes to regard Paul the missionary apostle as a person who basically remained within the framework of the Pharisaic faith in which he had been cradled and trained.[5] It is beyond the scope of this discussion to interact with the other alternative approaches to the background material. W. D. Davies (1980) and E. P. Sanders (1977) have adequately demonstrated the weaknesses of the other positions and the strengths of the rabbinic interpretation.[6]

The Spirit's activity was basically regarded as a past phenomenon in Israel's history, a phenomenon which had indeed given to Israel its Torah, its prophets, and the whole of its Scriptures, but had ceased when the prophetic office ended. Yet, there were individuals who were conscious of the Holy Spirit as still active in their lives. Davies suggests that Paul was reared within a Judaism that tended to relegate the Spirit's activities to the past (1980: 215). It was, however, a Judaism that cherished a strong expectation of the coming of the Holy Spirit in the future. Paul was a Jew who believed that the

4. So Cullmann 1951: 26. When I use the term *systematic theology*, I refer to the technical sense of that term as a discipline that treats materials in a systematic fashion under the categories of "Theology Proper," "Christology," etc. This is not to deny the proper place of systematic theology nor to deny that Paul is a theologian or that his writings can be considered theology in that they are reflections upon the words and acts of God.

5. There is another line of interpretation that sees Paul's thought based in the mystical influences of the Greco-Roman world. This view has been characteristically associated with Rudolf Bultmann.

6. See the descriptive summary of these points in Martin 1981: 9:31. Cf. also Kim 1982.

Messiah had come in Jesus of Nazareth and thus regarded the Messianic Age as the promised age of the Spirit.

This being the case, the apostle maintained certain expectations which would accompany the coming of the age of the Spirit. In becoming a Christian, Paul entered a new community, and in the pneumatic power that characterized its enthusiasm, he observed evidence of the advent of the age to come. The active presence of the Spirit was a mark of the last days. The ministry of the Spirit authenticated the claims of Jesus as Messiah. As Davies comments, Paul's eschatological expectations regarding the age of the Spirit were confirmed through observation and experience. He emphasizes that

> the awareness of the Supernatural Power at work in the community, which issued in ecstatic experiences and in a fruitful moral enthusiasm, phenomena which cannot be paralleled in the contemporary Judaism, at any rate to anything like the same degree, would be taken by Paul as evidence that he had arrived at the Age when it was bliss to be alive and very heaven to be young. We are far removed from the individualistic, esoteric pneumatology of the Hellenistic world and in the full stream of that Rabbinic thought which had looked forward to a community and an Age of the Spirit. For Paul, with the advent of Christ, this had arrived (Davies 1980: 217).

Before I focus on the primary texts, I would like to look at another passage that might give a hint of Paul's early experience in the age of the Spirit.

Spirit in Paul's Experience.   The expected ecstatic and enthusiastic experiences of the age of the Spirit were personally witnessed by Paul, as he claims in 2 Cor 12:1–10. He mentions an event fourteen years earlier which would place it before any of the extant writings.[7] We know that it is Paul's autobiographical experience because of v. 7, even though it initially appears to be an account of someone else because of the third-person usage. Paul uses the third person to distance himself and his apostolic identity from the self in which he had been forced to boast (Baird 1985: 653–54). The Corinthian "super apostles" evidenced characteristics of ecstatics who claimed divine inspiration. Their apostolate was grounded not only in miracles but also in impressive feats like ecstasy and visions (2 Cor 12:1, 5:12–13). They accused Paul of being fleshly (2 Cor 10:2), weak, and without

7. One must recognize that this experience lacks explicit reference to Spirit. It seems quite possible that his reference to "in Christ" is similar or equal to "in Spirit" (see Davies 1980: 177–78).

courage (2 Cor 10:21, 11:7). As Baird notes, Paul uses the "third person to prove that his ministry is not grounded in the sort of experience they claim as normative" (1985: 654). He uses his weakness to confront their supposed strengths (Dunn 1977b: 191).

Paul did not relate whether or not he saw the risen Lord, but he did tell the readers that he heard the Lord (v. 4). The experience brought him to the inner compartment of the third heaven, paradise (v. 4).[8] Here he heard unutterable words (ἄρρητα ῥήματα), but, unlike some of the marvelous details of contemporary apocalyptic literature, Paul gives no information of what he heard, for it was impermissible for him to talk about it (v. 4) (Baird 1985: 659).

Paul had experienced the event earlier and mentions it now as a maturing apostle. If this mystical experience informs Paul's readers of his early encounter with the Spirit, then it describes a pneumatic experience that lacks parameters and shape. In his ongoing apostolic pilgrimage, Paul developed a different understanding of this event so as to deprecate it, as evidenced by the passage. I now turn attention to the apostle's teaching concerning life in the Spirit by considering the texts in their traditionally understood chronological order.

The Spiritual Life in the Teaching of Paul

Galatians 5:13–16.   Galatians includes Paul's polemical defense of his apostleship and his explanation of the relation between the Law and the Spirit. The Gentile believers were invited to engage themselves with the Law in a way that Paul prohibited. The passage under investigation exhorts the Galatians to live/walk by the Spirit and not to follow the fleshly desires characteristic of those outside the believing community.[9]

In these brief notations, my focus will be directed toward vv. 16, 18, and 25. These references are not precisely parallel, but in v. 16 and v. 18 a contrast is made to emphasize an action characterized as "by the Spirit" (πνεύματι). The exhortation in v. 16 is an active construction with an instrumental dative, indicating walking by the Spirit. The verb in v. 18 is passive in form, again with the dative con-

8. See 2 Cor 5:13. Also note Hughes 1962: 432–33, who cites Calvin's suggestion that "three" is used because it points to completion or perfection. See also Barrett 1973 and Scholem 1965 and 1961.

9. The question of date or origin seems to matter little for my purposes. At this point I am in agreement with Betz 1979: 12—that it is an early rather than later document. Yet, Betz opts for a north Galatian setting rather than an earlier date accompanying a southern setting, as suggested by Bruce 1970–71; cf. Davies 1984: 172–75, whose corrective comments on the situation at Galatia are very helpful.

struction meaning being led by the Spirit. The two ideas are very similar and each is illumined by the other. Walking by the Spirit means not gratifying the desires of the flesh, while being led by the Spirit is the opposite of being under Law. The exhortation in v. 18 establishes parameters for life in the Spirit by establishing opposition to fleshly license, and v. 18 excludes legalism as a guide for the believer. The enablement supplied by the Spirit thus excludes both legalism and license. Legalism and license are further defined by the household lists which distinguish the virtues of those in the believing community assisted by the Spirit from the vices characteristic of those who do not have the Spirit's assistance (Schweizer 1979). As E. D. Burton notes on v. 16, desires (ἐπιθυμίαι) and the flesh (σάρξ) emphasize "the contrast in character between the Spirit-controlled type of life and that which is governed by the impulse of the flesh" (1920: 298).

The listing of the fruit of the Spirit in vv. 22–23 gives the positive shape to the spiritual life which contrasts the negative shape provided by the vice lists of vv. 19–21. In v. 25 the apostle gives a summary verse for this section with the repetition of the phrase *by the Spirit* providing strong emphasis so that it can be understood as an exhortation to "keep in step with the Spirit" (Packer 1984: 94–120). H. N. Ridderbos comments:

> This short statement [has] unusual force. It proceeds from a definite assumption (*If we live by the Spirit . . .*), the truth of which must prove itself (*by the Spirit let us also walk*). The first points out the principial relation to the Spirit. . . . The second clause speaks of the activity of believers which they exercise in the strength of the new principle granted them (Ridderbos 1953: 210).

The emphasis of the context, as discussed by David Lull (1980), is upon the Spirit's power for motivation and enablement in living. Verse 25 summarizes this section: "Since we live by the Spirit, let us also walk by the Spirit." Paul's view of life in the Spirit is characterized by power that enables and motivates for life. His view of life in the Spirit develops shape in both positive and negative ways. This is accomplished for Paul by the lists of vices and virtues. The virtues are genuine examples of the ethical character produced in the one who walks by the Spirit.

1 Corinthians 12:14. In the setting of chaps. 12–14, Paul is addressing the problem of an enthusiastic spirituality that was out of control in Corinth, especially the confusion abounding regarding tongues-speaking and ecstatic experiences. Paul treats the need for discernment, the variety in the body, spiritual gifts, the supremacy of love, the superiority of prophecy, and the need for orderliness. There apparently were numerous misuses of the charismatic gifts in the community. The background is influenced by the mystery religions which were so prevalent in Corinthian culture.

It was widely accepted in antiquity that some people were in especially close touch with the divine and had special spiritual endowments. Usually this was understood in terms of trances and ecstatic speech. Since the day of Pentecost, there had been some within the church who manifested such spiritual gifts. While the Holy Spirit was given to all believers (Rom 8:9, 14) some received special gifts so that they did unusual things such as speaking in tongues. For many at Corinth, this activity was the hallmark of the spiritual person. By comparison, the household guidelines of Christian virtues seemed colorless. Paul's epoch-making discussion shows that the issue is primarily one of Lordship (12:3), not libertinism (Longsworth 1981). All spiritual gifts must be brought to this touchstone. If their exercise is inimical to Christ, they are not of God. He lists some of these gifts, but proceeds to the more excellent way of love (12:31ff.). Paul does not deny that spectacular gifts have a place. But he insists that the important thing is the manifestation of ethical qualities, especially love (ἀγάπη), which the presence of the Spirit in the heart of believers makes possible. The spectacular gifts are valuated in relation to the conduct of public worship, and he insists that all must be done "in a fitting and orderly way" (14:40). It is very clear that the apostle does not assign these gifts such a place of eminence as they were accorded in popular esteem.

Paul assumes that all Corinthians share in the gifts of the Spirit (12:4) and that all these gifts are for the common good (12:7) and the building up of the community (14:12). The concept of the edification of the spiritual body of Christ is primary in Paul's view of the place of the χαρίσματα in the church (14:13). The ministry of the body of Christ is a charismatic one and includes speaking gifts, leadership gifts, sign gifts, and helping gifts. It is important to remember the Spirit's work through the gifts that are seemingly less significant because "unless the church is built by this kind of unheralded labor, not one brick is put in place" (Baird 1980: 53; Dunn 1977b: 109–10).

The gift of the Spirit which is at the center of the Corinthian problem is the gift of tongues, or glossalalia. The person uttering this coveted gift would utter praises to God that were intelligible neither to the speaker nor to that person's hearer. The person speaking experienced great exaltation of spirit but had no rational

communication of the will of God (14:14), as did the prophets. The
experience was meaningless to the hearers unless a gift of interpretation was given (14:13) that could communicate the message in rational terms. The Corinthians apparently believed that tongues were
the superior gift, and the excesses in the exercise of this gift had introduced disorder and strife in the church. Paul maintains that personal ecstasy is not the goal, but rather the edification of all. The
guidelines include no more than two or three speaking in a single
meeting, and only then in turn, and only if someone is present to
interpret. Tongues are subordinate to prophecy, but prophetic utterance must also be conducted in an orderly manner (14:29) (Ladd
1974: 536). The gifts are sovereignly given for the edification of the
community, and thus it is impossible to predict when and where
they will be manifested. Since some of the supernatural gifts were
associated with apostles and prophets for the foundation of the
church (cf. Eph 2:20), it is possible that some of the gifts were particularly for the apostles.

Paul develops guidelines in this context which give shape to the
corporate view of the spiritual life. These guidelines can be summarized by the statement in 1 Cor 14:40 exhorting that "all things be
done in a fitting and orderly way." This phrase governs the entire
spectrum of the activities of the believing community. The basis for
this theme is found in the very character of God (14:33): "God is not
a God of disorder, but of peace."

Guiding principles are required for this theme of order and
peace to be exercised in the community. At this point, tension is created in Paul's view of the Christian life founded upon freedom
(Bruce 1978: 82–86). Nevertheless, even in the exercise of such principles, there is an absence of legalism in Paul's approach. In the text,
the constraints concern the true and false prophets (14:29–30). The
spirits of the prophets were subject to the prophets themselves and
were to be tested by all who confessed Jesus as Lord (12:3) (Conzelmann 1975: 245). The Corinthian emphasis is placed upon the
edification of the community and the correcting of triumphalism
and ecstatic experiences that were out of control in Corinth. The
concept of the Spirit is given shape in the community by the establishment of guiding principles. This is accomplished through the en-
dowing of the church with apostles and prophets to establish
principles concerning the order of the church. In the lists of gifts in
chap. 12, we can observe the consistent priority given to the gift of
apostle. In contrast to this, tongues and the interpretation of
tongues are listed last in these same lists. This is indicative of the

norms being developed in the community. The argument shows that
true spirituality is evidenced by love (12:31ff.) and unity (12:13) and
is established upon the touchstone of lordship (12:3), not ecstatic experiences. Paul for the first time gives guidelines for the exercise of
the corporate spiritual life. These guidelines differ from the list of
vices and virtues in that the guidelines for the Corinthians are for
those who share life in the Spirit, whereas lists of vices characterize
those outside the sphere of the Spirit. The shape of the spiritual life
is personalized by the giving of the gifts for the community.

2 Corinthians 3:7–18.   Paul addresses the issue of letter and Spirit
and the differences between the two, as well as the relation of believers within the covenant community of faith to the new covenant. He
describes the significant role of the Spirit in the new covenant. In the
new covenant, the Spirit is the inward ruling principle of life in contrast with the Law, which was the outward ruling principle of the Mo-
saic age. The Jewish legalists magnifying the Law are the adversaries
in the situation being addressed. Paul offers his credentials in 3:1–3
and expounds the difference beween letter and Spirit. The glory of
the new covenant is detailed in vv. 7–18, with an emphatic description
found in vv. 17–18 of the characteristics of the age of the Spirit.

The Spirit is the agent that brought conversion to the Corinthians.
This work of the Spirit ushered them into participation in the new
covenant (v. 6) (Barrett 1973: 108). The newness of the covenant compared with the old is that the Spirit who gives life is now substituted for
a written code that kills. Verses 7–18 expound the superiority of the
new over the old by comparing the splendor or glory which it imparts,
and offers an explanation for the basis and means of the transfer from
old to new (Hamilton 1957: 4). The splendor of the old covenant was
a fading one (3:7), in fact, it had faded away (3:10). In contrast, the
splendor of the dispensation of the Spirit is one which transforms its
beholders into ever-increasing glory (ἀπὸ δόξης εἰς δόξαν, 3:18).

This contrast is presented by a Pauline commentary on Exod
34:29–35 in order to establish that the proclamation of the gospel is
attended by even greater glory than the giving of the Law. When
Moses came down from Sinai with the tablets of the Law, his face
shone because he had been talking with God face to face, so much
so that the Israelites could not look at his face.

The fading of the glory on Moses' face is inferred from Exod
34:33, which states that Moses' face was recharged with glory every
time he went into the presence of Yahweh in the tent of meeting.

The future aspect of the question in v. 8 ("will not the ministry of the Spirit be even more glorious?") is logical, not necessarily chronological. The Spirit is given to those who receive the message.

The contrast is clearly seen by demonstrating that the service of Moses condemns the lawbreaker, while the ministry of the Spirit, which comes through the apostle's proclamation, brings about righteousness. What Moses received by way of glory was and remained limited in this matter, in that Moses did not yet have the ministry of the Spirit and of righteousness but was entrusted only with the ministry of condemnation and of death. In v. 12, Paul begins his summary statement, introduced by "therefore," which is grounded in his comments in vv. 10–11. The Law was transient, but the new covenant is permanent and cannot be outshone. The hope that belongs to recipients of the Spirit springs from the assurance of the unfading glory of the gospel which Paul and the other apostles were commissioned to proclaim (Bruce 1971: 120).

The inability of the Israelites to look at the glory in Moses' face (v. 14), fading though that glory was, is treated as a parallel of their descendants' present inability to realize the transitory character of the age of the Spirit. The intensive adversative (ἀλλά) suggests that, even to the present hearers, the Torah contained truth, but it could not penetrate the veil to the heart. The veil can be removed by believing in the Lord, and one can experience God in a personal way as did Moses in Exodus 34. This is the significance of the Spirit's work in the new covenant.

Verse 17 brings us to what is perhaps Paul's most striking statement regarding the Spirit, in which he in some way equates the Spirit with the resurected Lord. Davies comments (1980: 177) that through "the Resurrection Christ had become the life-giving Spirit, and so the Christian who is ἐν χριστῷ [in Christ] can also be described in a parallel fashion as being ἐν πνεύματι [in Spirit]."[10] Paul's functional statement stresses that the Spirit is the one who communicates the benefits of the new covenant by universalizing the work of Jesus and brings the ascended Lord to earth again.

God's Law is written by the Spirit on the hearts of believers. The believer is not bound by a legalistically conceived religion but now lives in the sphere of the Spirit, which is characterized by freedom. Freedom is freedom from the Law and from sin, as well as freedom to obedience.

---

10. In Paul's writings there is, however, an ambiguity concerning the relationship of Christ and the Spirit. In 2 Cor 3:17 we find not only "Lord in Spirit," but also "Spirit of the Lord." See also Rom 8:9.

The Spirit is transforming the members of the believing community into the likeness of the Lord. This work is a very personalized approach to the Spirit (3:3, 8). Paul is not without a theology of glory and indeed has his own kind of paradoxical triumphalism (Barrett 1973: 126). Paul has revealed the personal side of the Spirit that is nevertheless a transforming power that reveals the glory and superiority of the new covenant and the age of the Spirit. The superiority of the new covenant is clearly demonstrated through a closely reasoned, yet loose, exegesis of Exodus 34.

2 Corinthians 12:1–10. This passage is set within the boundaries of chaps. 10–13, a portion of the letter often identified as the "severe" or "sorrowful letter." Paul sets forth his apostolic authority against the "super apostles." In the preceding context (11:30–33), he relates the account of his basket experience that brought about his escape from Damascus. The passage is followed by Paul's description of the marks of an apostle (12:11ff.).

We have already viewed the ecstatic experience of the apostle which he mentions in this passage. The amazing thing is not that Paul had such a mystical experience, but that he deprecates it. He evaluates his experience of exaltation into heaven, as he does speaking in tongues (1 Cor 14:19) and other ecstatic experiences (2 Cor 5:13), in his relation to his service to the church.[11] Paul does not want his ministry evaluated by these types of experiences.

Paradoxically, he points to marks of apostleship, not as ecstatic phenomena, but as weakness and suffering. The only valid and visible sign of apostolicity was the weakness the apostle was prepared to accept so that the power of Christ might be manifested in him.

Paul refrains from boasting because he does not wish his readers (v. 6) to take him at his own evaluation (v. 8), but on the basis of their personal experience. In vv. 7–10, Paul rejoices in his tribulation because a scene of human weakness is the best possible stage for the display of divine power. It remains a mystery exactly how we are to understand the thorn (v. 7) (Barrett 1973: 314–17). All that can be explained about this situation is that Paul was afflicted with a painful malady that affected his ministry (Baird 1985: 661). The ministry in which he was engaged was somehow illumined for him through that weakness. The realization of this fact makes him glory

11. Andrew T. Lincoln (1981: 72) comments that even though Paul's reference to these enthusiastic types of events are few, it does not mean a lack of frequent experience. Paul seems to make the event public only when forced to do so by his opponents.

in his weakness, if it is by this means that the power of Christ rests upon him. Paul solves the problem of the superior strength and superior experiences of the "super apostles" by countering them with his weakness and his account of an experience very similar to those of the "super apostles" (Spittler 1975: 265). Paul's view of the spiritual life develops further shape through reflection upon this experience. Life in the Spirit is a life of obedience in suffering service.

Romans 7–8. These important chapters describe the Christian life in its struggle, its present and eschatological tension, and its freedom especially in its reflection to the Law's inability to accomplish what can be accomplished by the Spirit. Traditionally, the Book of Romans has been perceived as a summary of Paul's theology.[12] Philip Melancthon (1532 [1965]) characterized Romans as a *compendium doctrinae Christiane.* This approach assumes that Paul had never traveled to Rome prior to the writing of this epistle, and thus it is written as a foundational document to ground the Roman church in its new faith. Thus, Romans is considered a summary of Paul's sytstematized theology.

There are certainly many strengths in such a view, but it lacks the dynamic so characteristic of the NT. G. Bornkamm has argued carefully and persuasively for a contextual understanding of Romans (1971: 88–96). The purpose of such an effort would have been to win the approval of the Jerusalem church and to seek the unity in the church Paul desired before going west with the gospel. While it is impossible to be dogmatic concerning any reconstruction of the life situation of the Roman correspondence, the suggestions by Bornkamm are inviting.

The history of the interpretation of Romans 7 is lengthy and varied. Recognizing the various options, following Cranfield (1975–79), Barrett (1957) and Murray (1959), I see this chapter as an autobiographical account of Paul's struggle with the Law and with indwelling sin.[13] A number of indications in the letter might lead the reader to infer that the Law is actually evil, in some way and equal to sin (5:20, 6:14). Paul seeks to correct and deal with these possible

---

12. This approach was first advanced by Philip Melancthon in 1532 (see Melancthon 1965). The best representation of this approach is C. Hodge 1866. Also, several recent works have adopted this interpretation (see Bruce 1977: 326 and Keck 1979: 15). It must be acknowledged that Romans comes very close to a systematic treatment of theological themes.

13. The numerous interpretations for this passage are outlined in Cranfield 1975: 343–44.

false conclusions. Verses 7–13 present three stages in Paul's preconversion relation to the Law:

1. the period of ignorance and innocence (v. 7)
2. the period of awakening to his inability to keep the Law (vv. 8–9)
3. the period of death and condemnation (vv. 10–13)

The central lesson to be learned from this section is that the Law can command what to do, but cannot impart the power to carry out its injunctions.

Paul paints a picture of a state of distress, but not of hopelessness, in vv. 14–25. It is a lifelong struggle that Paul outlines and typifies. Verse 25 points to an eschatological hope. The present tenses and high recognition of Law point to Paul as a maturing believer. Paul speaks for all who have need of God's constant enablement and blessing. The tension of the struggle, the paradox of life and death must be maintained to the end. It is a picture of Paul's already/not yet tension of the spiritual life. Verse 24 is the lifelong cry of frustration, v. 25a is an offer of thanksgiving for the eschatological hope, and v. 25b is the expression of the apostle's realism (Dunn 1975: 270).

Paul moves in chap. 8 to address the function of the Spirit in the life of the believer in both its present and eschatological senses. The main subject of 8:1–27 is that life promised for the person who is righteous by faith is one characterized by the indwelling Spirit of God.

The "now" (ἄρα νῦν) in 8:1 is a connective with 7:6. The reference is not to some moment of conversion, thought of as having occurred between v. 24 and v. 25a of chap. 7, but to the gospel events themselves: "Now since Christ has died and been raised from the dead." In Christ, believers share in his death and shall pass with him in resurrection into the age to come. Verse 2 describes further liberation in Christ by the life-giving Spirit. The first and primary function of the Spirit in this age is to give life. The Spirit produces life just as Law and sin produce death. Liberation could only come through a new and creative act of God (Barrett 1957: 158).

Verses 5–11 amplify v. 4 concerning what it means to walk "according to Spirit" (κατὰ πνεῦμα), that is, to demonstrate a lifestyle (περιπατοῦντες) characterized by the Spirit. Life according to Spirit is contrasted with life according to flesh (σάρξ). C. K. Barrett accurately reflects that to be characterized by flesh in the world is inevitably to cut oneself off from the source of life and therefore to court death (1957: 158–59). Flesh has negative characteristics and means disobedience and exclusion from God.

Verse 9 is significant, for in it believers are not characterized by flesh, but by Spirit. Barrett notes:

> Paul is in process of developing a new definition of the Christian life. When he speaks of dying and rising with Christ, and of justification, he is using terms eschatological in origin; now he speaks of the Spirit, contrasting the invisible activity of God himself with the visible world of the flesh. Christians are men whose lives are directed from a source outside themselves (Barrett 1957: 158).

Hence the definition offered by Paul: "If anyone does not have the Spirit of Christ, he does not belong to Christ." The purpose of this statement is ultimately positive in that it asserts that every true believer is Spirit indwelt.

Life in the Spirit is also Christologically grounded. The Spirit of God and the Spirit of Christ are the same person of Spirit. The believer in Christ is in the Spirit, and the believer indwelt by Christ is indwelt by the Spirit. In some sense, vv. 10–11 preview vv. 18–27. Paul's thought is that, through the indwelling of the Spirit, Christ is himself present to us, the indwelling of the Spirit being the manner of Christ's dwelling in believers. It is this indwelling Spirit that gives life to the community of believers (8:10).

The resurrection event of Christ was an eschatological act (Rom 6:4) which marked the beginning of the age to come. The resurrection event was the pledge of the eschaton and was connected by the presence and activity of the Holy Spirit, who brings the life-giving activity of God to bear upon every stage of the intervening period so that even our mortal bodies are transformed and quickened (Käsemann 1980: 224–25).

In vv. 12–17, Paul declares that the eschatological glory is guaranteed by the present operation of the Spirit. It is only by the Spirit that the flesh can be overcome so as to participate in the eschatological life. If persons live by the flesh, they will die. The construction in v. 13 is a periphrastic future, with emphasis on the consequences of a flesh-dominated life. The flesh produces activities of scheming, human self-centeredness, and self-assertion. This is in contrast with those who are led by the Spirit, directed by the Spirit, or driven by the Spirit—in more enthusiastic terms, who are true heirs of God. They have received the promise of adoption, and their future salvation is guaranteed. Thus, they are children of God.[14]

---

14. *Children of God* is a rare expression for Paul, but it is not to be equated with the Johannine concept of regeneration.

Those who have been adopted and who have received the gift of the Spirit are ushered into a relationship with God as personal father (cf. Gal 4:6, Mark 14:36). The emphasis upon a *personal* relationship is similar to the expression of seeing "face to face" in 2 Cor 3:16–18. The adopted child can now cry out in a Spirit–inspired prayer, "Abba! Father!" (cf. 1 Cor 14:15).

The Spirit, having been given to God's children, bears witness with their own spirit of the truth of their adoption. This must not be reduced to individualistic expressions, but must be seen in the true sense of community witness (Ridderbos 1975: 199–204). As children, believers are more than heirs to the promises of Abraham (Galatians 3, Romans 4), but are coheirs with Christ. Paul declares, "when we suffer with him, we may be glorified together with him." The process initiated in common suffering cannot but end in common glory.

The final section of chap. 8 (vv. 18–27) addresses the interim period prior to the consummation of the kingdom, which is characterized by suffering. Paul explains how the spiritual community can take courage from the prospect of glory and from the assistance already given them by the Holy Spirit. The entire world (v. 19) "strains its neck" (ἀποκαραδοκία) looking for the eschatological revelation (cf. 1 Cor 1:7). Creation is subject to bondage and vanity; the whole universe needs redemption from the present struggle. Paul seemingly personifies this bondage which is inevitably corrupting. Over against this corrupting bondage stands the eschatological liberation of the glory of God's children. Out of this glory comes Paul's emphasis upon freedom from death, sin, and corruption.

Paul represents this time (νῦν), the "not yet" aspect of the present, as a time of groaning. Creation can do nothing but wait and hope and groan. The advantage of the believing community during this time is that it has the Spirit as it waits, hopes, and groans. The Spirit is described as the firstfruits, the first installment, a pledge of final deliverance. The Holy Spirit is thus regarded as an anticipation of final salvation and a pledge that those who have the Spirit shall in the end be saved. A very important point is that the possession of the Spirit is a great privilege, but it is not God's final gift for which the faithful community still eagerly looks forward. Adoption is the final acceptance, which is the time of bodily redemption. This understanding means that the members of the church must put no confidence in themselves, but look steadily beyond themselves, through the gift of the Spirit, to find the fulfillment of their own selves and actions in God. Paul characteristically uses the future tense in regard to salvation, but in v. 24, he uses the aorist tense (ἐσώθημεν); yet the future is certainly indicated by the phrase *in hope* (ἐλπίδι), possibly to be translated "until then." "In hope" represents an attitude of expectant waiting that belongs to the church because of the gift of the Spirit (v. 25).

The conclusion of the Spirit's activity in the midst of the struggle is illustrated by Paul through the example of the believer's prayer life (8:26). Paul chooses this example because prayer is the most basic of religious duties.[15] But there is more to it than even this obvious observation. The idea is directly related to unutterable words (cf. 2 Corinthians 12). Käsemann (1980: 240–41) sees this expression of prayer as similar to the ecstatic experiences of 1 Corinthians 12 and 14. It seems better, however, to see Paul's reference to prayer as meaning the activity of the Spirit. The Spirit actually makes intercession for the believer (MacRae 1980: 288). The Spirit points to the ultimate security in God of those whom God has chosen. The presence of the Spirit, the firstfruits, is a proof that the age to come has dawned and that its consummation cannot long be delayed.

We have seen in these two important chapters of Romans how Paul shows that life in the Spirit is life giving. He points to the need for the enablement of the Spirit in the community's struggle with indwelling sin and ongoing suffering. Paul develops the themes of "in Christ" and "in Spirit" to their fullest canonical shape. He shows that the Spirit is very personal, a gift, a down payment of the eschaton when struggle will end. The present age in which believers participate in life in the Spirit is an ongoing process toward maturity, moving away from a superficial triumphalism to a genuine eschatological glory. It is the Spirit who provides hope for the community of believers during this interim period of struggle.

Paul's view of the spiritual life developed from early in his ministry to his mature understanding of enablement, which he explicated later in his pilgrimage. This view developed in its shape in such a way that it cannot be viewed as a pneumatic experience lacking parameters. It is life that is shaped by the lists of virtues and vices and by the guidelines given for the exercise of spiritual gifts in the corporate community. This concept of the spiritual life moved toward a personal understanding of the Spirit as one who provides comfort and assistance in the midst of struggle and suffering.

---

15. Käsemann (1980: 240–41) suggests the relationship of this passage to the glossalalia discussion elsewhere in Paul. Cf. Wedderburn 1975: 369, who thinks that Käsemann's view is doubtful. Also see MacRae 1980: 288; Mitchell 1982: 232; Bloesch 1980; and Grenz 1988.

Developmental/Contextual Considerations

Scholastic Approach

In my introductory comments, I noted various options for understanding the variety of Paul's teaching concerning the spiritual life.
The first view, representative of scholastic theology, pictures Paul as
a theologian applying his theology with different emphases in different contexts. This position is uncomfortable, speaking of Paul in
developmental terms, although a careful acknowledgment of progressive revelation within the writings would be affirmed. Change of
emphases in the epistles is noted, but not development of doctrine.
It is believed, according to this view, that the apostle's theology was
fully developed from the first stroke of his pen. The development
that we have observed in Paul's view of the spiritual life is much
more dynamic than what is commonly advocated among scholastic
theologians.

Existential Approach

A second view is generally associated with Rudolf Bultmann. This
position has dominated NT scholarship during the middle of the
twentieth century. This particular understanding of development emphasizes the innovations in the growth of doctrine and minimizes any
necessary propositional connection with the foundational core. It
stresses changes that have brought about innovative, even contradictory, reformations of Christian thought. According to the Bultmannian approach, Paul's diversity is seen as a model of existential
Christian theology with its insistence on the historically unconnected,
momentary nature of God's encounter with humankind. For example,
Bultmann draws attention to the considerable diversity of theological
interests and ideas in the earliest period, and points out that a norm
for doctrine is lacking throughout this period. He suggests:

> In the beginning, *faith* is the term which distinguishes the Christian
> Congregation from Jews and the heathen, not *orthodoxy* (right doc-
> trine). The latter along with its correlate, *heresy*, arises out of the
> differences which develop within the Christian congregations (Bult-
> mann 1955: 2.135).

As applied to Paul's thought, this viewpoint can be clearly seen in
Bultmann's review of the second edition of Karl Barth's *Epistle to
the Romans*. Bultmann charged that Barth's commentary was in-
sufficiently critical of Paul, for in Paul there are other spirits speak-

ing besides the πνεῦμα χριστοῦ (spirit of Christ), such as the Jewish, the popular Christian, the Hellenistic, and others.[16]

Bultmann believed that Martin Heidegger accurately and fully traced out the categories defining the possibilities of human experience in his masterful work *Being and Time* (1927). Bultmann demythologizes Jesus and Paul by conforming what they thought to these categories. In doing so, Bultmann is not letting the NT texts speak for themselves, nor is he open to the possibilities of human existence that the NT texts, rather than Heidegger, set forth (Dunn 1977a). Similarly, Wolfhart Pannenberg comments:

> Although there is no intention of dimming down the particular content of the text (in Bultmann), but rather of making it visible precisely for contemporary understanding, nevertheless that content is narrowed down from the outset: anything other than the possibilities of human existence cannot become relevant for existential interpretation. . . . Now, it is rather doubtful that the text which is to be interpreted on the basis of such handling can still say what it has to say on its own: the New Testament texts, for example, are concerned, at least explicitly, with many things other than the possibilities of understanding human existence, although everything with which they are concerned will also be an element of the understanding of the existence of the New Testament author (Pannenberg 1967: 132).

It seems that the great diversity seen in the development of the NT texts is brought to the text by Bultmann. The picture of development observed in Paul is less diverse and demonstrates both a foundational core and genuine continuity.

Contextual Approach

The third approach to understanding Paul traces the development in the apostle's thought to contextual considerations. This view is associated with J. C. Beker and his work *Paul the Apostle* (1980). In his comprehensive presentation of this approach, Beker maintains that the coherent theme of Paul's thought is the apocalyptic triumph of God in the imminent redemption of the created order which has been inaugurated in Christ. Moreover, he sees Paul's hermeneutic as translating the apocalyptic theme of the gospel into the contingent particularities of the human situation. It is this inability to correlate the consistent theme of the gospel and its contingent relevance that constitutes Paul's unique achievement in the

---

16. This material is assembled in Robinson 1968: 1.120–27.

history of early Christian thought. In the contextual application of his central coherent theme, Paul neither imposes a theological system on his hearers nor compromises the truth of the gospel for the sake of strategic victory, nor does he celebrate spiritual immediacy at the price of consistency. While I think that there is greater development than that seen by Beker, he is correct in pointing to Paul's changing context as a major aspect and motivation for the development that takes place in the apostle's ongoing maturity.

Continuity Approach

The fourth view, which I believe is more comprehensive than the three positions just surveyed, speaks of both continuity with a foundational core and genuine growth in conceptualization and expression. This was the approach of the Antiochian Fathers and "has come to characterize the methodology of the more constructive theologians of our day, whatever their particular confessional stance" (Longenecker 1984: 25). It is a model that appeals by way of analogy to the relationship between a growing plant and its original seed, and which argues that real growth always involves genuine innovations of structure but that growth is always controlled by what is inherent in the seed itself. The developments are somewhat like a series of branches, to be sure often intertwined, growing out of the trunk of the unifying center. It recognizes that the stalk, leaves, and flower of the plant are not just reproductions of the original seed. Longenecker offers another appropriate analogy:

> Better yet, the analogy could be of a young man fervently in love with a young woman, whose love may have numerous psychological and physiological presuppositions unrecognized by him and whose early love-letters may fail to express all that his heart and mind feel, but who, as he grows in understanding and draws on the stock of ideas available to him in his culture, comes over a period of time to be able to understand more adequately and to express more fully his love, together with its ramifications and implications. This is not to imply that theological development is always a continuous and culminative growth in only one direciton (1984: 26).

Of course, just as seeds (and love!) grow in spurts and in aberrant ways, so does theology. It seems that Paul's theological and ethical thought often develops in spurts, hence the apparent rapid development over a short time. It is also possible that the outworking of this thought may at times drift in aberrant ways among his readers, such as at Corinth, hence the need for directional shifts. This fourth position recognizes that the NT writings of the apostle Paul are not a textbook on systematic theology. Rather, they are an inspired record of God's revelation and redemption in Jesus Christ and the church's understanding of what all that means. Particularly as it relates to my subject matter, this position sees Paul's teaching as a reflection of the understanding of life in the Spirit and its meaning for believers in the new community of faith. It attempts to take seriously certain aspects of each of the other three positions. Similar to the first position, it sees the apostle's teaching as God's revelation for the church. It is not, however, a static revelation but a progressive one (Vos 1948: 5–6). It recognizes the strengths of Beker's thesis and therefore sees the development in Paul's theology influenced by the demands of his situation and context. While distancing itself from the Bultmannian position of diversity, this view does recognize that the writings of Paul are dynamic and developmental in nature. The primary difference between these two approaches is ultimately based upon diverse hermeneutical starting points. For Bultmann, the goal of interpretation is to understand the possibilities of human existence. I believe that the goal of interpretation is to understand what an author or the text in its context is saying as completely as possible. Therefore, I affirm that our task is to understand the apostle Paul's meaning in his historical context.

Conclusion

A developmental approach to Paul's thought is not possible unless one can determine the meaning of the text in its particular setting. I have attempted to interpret Paul's view of the spiritual life as it developed from early in his ministry to his more mature, developed view which he presented later in his ministry. Without restating all of my conclusions, I note summarily that Paul's view of the spiritual life developed toward a more personal understanding that leads to seeing the Spirit as the one who provides help, comfort, and enablement in the midst of life's struggles. This picture of the spiritual life also developed in its shape. This life is not a pneumatic experience without parameters, but is life shaped by lists of vices and virtues, by guidelines given by the exercise of spiritual gifts in the church's worship and ministry, by the teachings of Jesus, and by the imperative statements directed to the church to be carried out in the time of the already/not yet tension. It thus brings freedom to the believers in the community, a freedom unto obedience. These developments take place in the thought of the apostle as he matures in his own

own spiritual pilgrimage, as demanded when his context changes and as he is the recipient of progressive revelation from God to the faithful community. I want to affirm that Paul's meaning in his writings can be determined through dedicated effort to reach back and read him in his original context and setting. But because his is a canonical word for the community, we can also read Paul for the present members of the believing fellowship. We must maintain both of these horizons. We must see our project as characterized by two interrelated phases: (1) literary-historical analysis and (2) canonical-theological analysis. The first deals primarily with the external features of the text and the situation in which the text has been placed by its author(s). The second is concerned with the inner life of the text, that is, how the text impinges on the members of the community, past and present. In this view, the norms and principles essential to historical and literary methodologies are incorporated into the theological interpretations, serving to guide and oversee theological application. Our task, then, is to go there and back again: to go to the author's meaning in the historical situation before coming back again to speak to the present.

With the two principles of development and context, it is possible to see further developments or trajectories that took place in Pauline thought that I did not examine in the exegetical or theological section above. There is an unusual construction, with Lukan patterns, in Eph 5:18, where the readers are exhorted to "be filled with Spirit." It is contrasted with an uncontrollable experience which can be produced by drunkenness. "Be filled with Spirit" is an exhortation given to the worshiping congregation and resulting in praise, prayers, and mutual submission to one another (vv. 19–21). Again it can be seen that the spiritual life in the corporate sense in the church is not an out-of-control pneumatic experience but one that has shape and leads to worship patterns and ethical actions. The next step can perhaps be seen in the organizational and institutional patterns of the Pastoral Epistles. We must not think that trajectories are pre-set and inevitable. As Martin observes, "Even missiles are liable to mid-course corrections and are exposed to unforeseen forces" (1981: 4–5). We must allow for similar changes in ideological flight paths as well.

From my review of the four approaches to the concept of development in Pauline theology I conclude that a combination of factors best explains the variety in the apostle's thought. It was observed that a developmental approach to Paul's thought is not possible unless one can determine the meaning of the text in its particular setting. Paul still speaks by canonical authority to the issues and needs of the church at the end of the twentieth century. Where there is legalism to Law and bondage to sin, the Spirit brings freedom. Where there is libertinism and antinomianism, the Spirit gives shape to the Christian life. Where there is struggling and suffering, the Spirit provides enablement, blessing, and promise of future glory. Where there is immaturity and triumphalism, the Spirit reminds us of the need for authentic obedience. The Spirit brings to the community the reality of the "not yet" tension in which it now lives and exhorts the church to live obediently by living out what it is in Christ/Spirit. Finally, the Spirit gives openness to God in prayer and intercedes for the community as it struggles and suffers on this side of the eschaton. Still there remains a paradox. Liberty comes through struggling and obedience, and glory through suffering.

References

Baird, William
   1980   *1 Corinthians/2 Corinthians*. Atlanta: John Knox.
   1985   "Visions, Revelation and Ministry: Reflections on 2 Cor 12:1–5 and Gal 1:11–17." *Journal of Biblical Literature* 104:651–62.
Barrett, C. K.
   1957   *A Commentary on the Epistle to the Romans*. New York: Harper.
   1968   *A Commentary on the First Epistle to the Corinthians*. New York: Harper.
   1973   *A Commentary on the Second Epistle to the Corinthians*. New York: Harper.
Beker, J. Christiaan
   1980   *Paul the Apostle: the Triumph of God in Life and Thought*. Philadelphia: Fortress.
Betz, Hans Dieter
   1979   *Galatians: A Commentary on Paul's Letter to the Churches in Galatia*. Philadelphia: Fortress.
Black, David Alan
   1984   *Paul, Apostle of Weakness*. New York: Lang.
Bloesch, Donald G.
   1980   *The Struggle of Prayer*. San Francisco: Harper & Row.
Bornkamm, Gunther
   1971   *Paul*. Translated by D. M. G. Stalker. New York: Harper and Row.
Bruce, F. F.
   1970–71 "Galatia Problems, 3: The 'Other Gospel'." 53:253–71.
   1971   *1 and 2 Corinthians*. New Century Bible. Grand Rapids: Eerdmans.
   1977   *Paul: Apostle of the Heart Set Free*. Grand Rapids: Eerdmans.

1978   "'All Things to All Men': Diversity in Unity and Other Pauline Tensions." Pp. 82–99 in *Unity and Diversity in New Testament Theology: Essays in Honor of George E. Ladd.* Edited by R. A. Guelich. Grand Rapids: Eerdmans.

Bultmann, Rudolf
1955   *Theology of the New Testament.* 2 vols. Translated by Groebel. New York: Scribners.

Burton, E. D.
1920   *A Critical and Exegetical Commentary on the Epistle to the Galatians.* International Critical Commentary. New York: Scribners.

Conzelmann, Hans
1975   *1 Corinthians.* Translated by J. W. Leitch. Hermeneia. Philadelphia: Fortress.

Cranfield, C. E. B.
1975–79   *A Critical and Exegetical Commentary on the Epistle to the Romans.* 2 vols. International Critical Commentary. Edinburgh: T. & T. Clark.

Cullmann, Oscar
1951   *Christ and Time: The Primitive Christian Conception of Time and History.* Translated by F. Filson. Philadelphia: Fortress.

Davies, W. D.
1980   *Paul and Rabbinic Judaism.* Philadelphia: Fortress.
1984   *Jewish and Pauline Studies.* Philadelphia: Fortress.222

Dunn, James D. G.
1975   *Jesus and the Spirit.* Philadelphia: Westminster.
1977a   "Demytholigizing—The Problem of Myth in the New Testament." Pp. 285–307 in *New Testament Interpretation.* Edited by I. Howard Marshall. Grand Rapids: Eerdmans.
1977b   *Unity and Diversity in the New Testament.* Philadelphia: Westminster.

Fee, Gordon
1987   *The First Epistle to the Corinthians.* New International Commentary on the New Testament. Grand Rapids: Eerdmans.

Gaffin, Richard
1978   *The Centrality of the Resurrection.* Grand Rapids: Baker.

Grenz, Stanley
1988   *Prayer: The Cry for the Kingdom.* Peabody, Massachusetts: Hendrickson.

Hamilton, Neill Q.
1957   *The Holy Spirit and Eschatology in Paul.* Scottish Journal of Theology Occasional Papers 6. Edinburgh: Oliver & Boyd.

Harris, Murray J.
1971   "2 Corinthians 5:1–10: Watershed in Paul's Eschatology?" *Tyndale Bulletin* 22:33–40.

Hodge, Charles
1866   *A Commentary on the Epistle to the Romans.* Philadelphia: Claxton.

Hughes, P. E.
1962   *Paul's Second Epistle to the Corinthians.* Grand Rapids: Eerdmans.

Hurd, J. C., Jr.
  1965   *The Origin of 1 Corinthians.* London: SPCK.
Käsemann, E.
  1980   *Commentary on Romans.* Translated by G. Bromiley. Grand Rapids: Eerdmans.
Keck, Leander
  1979   *Paul and His Letters.* Philadelphia: Fortress.
Kim, Seyoon
  1982   *The Origin of Paul's Gospel.* Grand Rapids: Eerdmans.
Ladd, George E.
  1974   *A Theology of the New Testament.* Grand Rapids: Eerdmans.
Lincoln, Andrew T.
  1981   *Paradise Now and Not Yet.* Society for New Testament Studies Monograph Series 43. Cambridge: Cambridge University Press.
Longenecker, Richard N.
  1964   *Paul, Apostle of Liberty.* New York: Harper.
  1975   "Pauline Theology." Vol. 4: pp. 660–64 in *Zondervan Pictoral Encyclopedia of the Bible.* Edited by Merrill C. Tenney. Grand Rapids: Zondervan.
  1979   "On the Concept of Development in Pauline Thought." Pp. 195–207 in *Perspectives on Evangelical Theology.* Edited by Kenneth S. Kantzer and Stanley N. Gundry. Grand Rapids: Baker.
  1984   *New Testament Social Ethics.* Grand Rapids: Eerdmans.
Longsworth, William
  1981   "Ethics in Paul: The Shape of Christian Life and a Method of Moral Reasoning." *The Annual of the Society of Christian Ethics*: 29–56.
Lull, David
  1980   *Spirit in Galatia.* Chico: Scholars Press.
MacRae, George
  1980   "Romans 8:26–27." *Interpretation* 34:288–97.
Martin, Ralph P.
  1981   *Reconciliation.* Atlanta: John Knox.
Melancthon, Philip
  1965   *Romerbrief-Kommentar.* Melancthon's Werke in auswahl 5. Edited by R. Stupperich. Guttersloh: Bertelsmann.
Mitchell, Curtis
  1982   "The Holy Spirit's Intercessory Ministry." *Bibliotheca Sacra* 139:230–42.
Moule, C. F. D.
  1977   *The Origin of Christology.* Cambridge: Cambridge University Press.
Murray, John.
  1959   *The Epistle to the Romans.* 2 vols. New International Commentary on the New Testament. Grand Rapids: Eerdmans.
Packer, James I.
  1984   *Keep in Step with the Spirit.* Old Tappan, New Jersey: Revell.

Pannenberg, Wolfhart
1967   "Hermeneutics and Universal History." Pp. 132 in *History and Hermeneutics*. Translated by Robert Funk. Tübingen: Mohr/New York: Harper & Row.

Ramsay, William
1960   *The Cities of St. Paul: Their Influence on His Life and Thought*. Grand Rapids: Baker.

Ridderbos, H. N.
1953   *The Epistle of Paul to the Churches of Galatia*. New International Commentary on the New Testament. Grand Rapids: Eerdmans.
1975   *Paul: An Outline of His Theology*. Translated by John R. DeWitt. Grand Rapids: Eerdmans.

Robinson, James M. (ed.)
1968   *The Beginnings of Dialectic Theology*. 2 vols. Richmond: John Knox.

Ryrie, Charles C.
1959   *Biblical Theology of the New Testament*. Chicago: Moody.

Sabatier, A. S.
1896   *The Apostle Paul: A Sketch of the Development of His Doctrine*. Translated A. M. Hellier. London: Hodder & Stoughton.

Sanders, E. P.
1977   *Paul and Palestinian Judaism*. Philadelphia: Fortress.

Sanders, James A.
1984   *Canon and Community*. Philadelphia: Fortress.

Scholem, G.
1961   *Trends in Jewish Mysticism*. Rev. ed. New York: Jewish Theological Seminary.
1965   *Jewish Gnosticism, Merkabah Mysticism and Talmudic Tradition*. Rev. ed. New York: Jewish Theological Seminary.

Schweizer, Eduard
1979   "Traditional Ethical Patterns in the Pauline and Post-Pauline Letters and Their Development (Lists of Vices and House-tables)." Pp. 195–209 in *Text and Interpretation: Studies in the New Testament Presented to Matthew Black*. Edited by E. Best and R. M. Wilson. Cambridge: Cambridge University Press.

Spittler, Russell P.
1975   "The Limits of Ecstasy: An Exegesis of 2 Corinthians 12:1–10." Pp. 259–66 in *Current Issues in Biblical and Patristic Interpretation*: Edited by G. Hawthorne. Grand Rapids: Eerdmans.

Vos, Geerhardus
1948   *Biblical Theology: Old and New Testaments: Studies in Honor of Merrill C. Tenney*. Grand Rapids: Eerdmans.

Wedderburn, A. J.
1975   "Romans 8:26—Towards a Theology of Glossalalia." *Scottish journal of theology* 28:369–77.

Wiles, M. F.
1976   *The Divine Apostle: The Interpretation of St. Paul's Epistles in the Early Church*. Cambridge: Cambridge University Press.

The Discourse Structure of Philemon: A Study in Textlinguistics

David L. Allen

Dallas, Texas

Modern Linguistic Theory and Discourse Analysis

The Chomskyian revolution in linguistics had one glaring weakness: it failed to break away from its Bloomfieldian presupposition that the sentence was the highest level of linguistic consideration. As a result, the sentence as a linguistic unit was overemphasized without regard to context, thus eliminating the possibility of determinable structure (grammar) beyond the sentence level.

Modern linguistic theory is now recognizing that we may (and indeed must) talk about the structure of meaning beyond the sentence level, just as we can talk about the structure of clause and sentence. The name given to this branch of linguistic study is textlinguistics,[1] or, more familiarly, discourse analysis. Formerly the Cinderella of linguistics, discourse analysis has been recently elevated, if not to the position of princess, at least to that of lady-in-waiting.

---

1. For a helpful survey of the field and excellent bibliography see de Beaugrande and Dressler 1981.

77

In an attempt to show the rightful place of discourse analysis in the study of linguistics as a whole, we may view language as a two-story, split-level house. The basement of the house is linguistics proper—the study of the basic elements of communication such as phonology, morphology, grammar, etc. Most split-level houses have a basement entrance, but it is not the main entrance. The first floor of the house we may call discourse analysis. This is the linguistic study of the text as a whole. The main entrance to our house of language is normally the first floor since it is here that most people enter any given text they read. One reads an entire story, letter, article, etc. without meticulous analysis of the phonology and morphology of each word or the grammatical analysis of each sentence. Yet at any given point, the reader/hearer of a discourse may stop and engage in minute analysis in any of these areas. The top floor of our split-level, two-story house may be called text theory. This is the interdisciplinary intersection of such disciplines as psychology, sociology, anthropology, etc. in the study of texts. The post-Bloomfieldian era has seen a flurry of activity taking place on the first and second floors of the house of language.

Discourse analysis offers those of us interested in biblical exegetics one of the most exciting, challenging, and fruitful methodological frontiers on the contemporary linguistic landscape. Yet despite the progress discourse studies have made in the last thirty years, OT and NT scholars alike have been, with few exceptions, reluctant to employ it.[2] One is hard pressed to find a recent commentary which approaches the text from a discourse perspective.

2. See Erickson 1983 for an excellent discussion of the present state of affairs. Several linguists have seen to it that commentators are not without the tools to practice discourse analysis. John Beekman and John Callow's *Translating the Word of God* (1974) and *The Semantic Structure of Written Communication* (1981) present a model for discourse analysis that has been widely used by the Wycliffe Bible Translators' Summer Institute of Linguistics. *Translating the Word of God* was one of the earliest works available to the biblical scholar which sought to analyze the larger semantic units of a biblical text, but because of its title it has been greatly neglected (interestingly enough, the foreword was written by J. Harold Greenlee). Wilbur Pickering's *Framework for Discourse Analysis* (1978) offers a discourse analysis of Colossians. He presently serves as a translation consultant at SIL, and in the preface to his book he acknowledges his debt to Beekman, Callow, Longacre, and others. Timothy and Barbara Friberg, also associated with Wycliffe Bible Translators, served as editors for the *Analytical Greek New Testament* (1981), an important work which provides a grammatical tag for every word of the Greek New Testament. These tags provide the exegete with linguistic information essential for determining the discourse function of large sections of text. The value of their work will be illustrated in my analysis of Philemon. J. P. Louw 1982) presents a method of colon analysis not unlike the propositional approach of the Beekman-Callow model. Likewise, Nida, Louw, Snyman, and Cronje (1983) provide the methodological tools for

Discourse Theory of Robert Longacre

Robert Longacre, a colleague of J. Harold Greenlee, has taught linguistics at the University of Texas at Arlington since 1972 and, having been an international field consultant for SIL, has applied discourse analysis to numerous languages with fruitful results. The purpose of this article is to apply the specific tagmemic[3] method/model of discourse analysis as developed by Longacre to the hortatory text of Philemon in an attempt to explicate its structure and macrostructure. Paul's epistle furnishes a classic example of the way an author makes use of mitigation in attempting to impose a course of action upon someone else.

Space does not permit a thorough analysis of Longacre's approach to discourse (see bibliography for his major works).[4] However, a summary would be in order. The foundation of the tagmemic model is twofold: (1) the notion of the distinction between function-slot and filler-set, and (2) the integrating of the two into a functional unit called the tagmeme (Longacre 1983b: 270). From this base, Longacre develops a model of discourse analysis which posits the following three aspects for any discourse: constituency structure, texture, and macrostructure.

First, all texts have constituency structure, that is, they are composed of paragraphs, sentences, clauses, and phrases. Longacre's brand of tagmemics does away with intermediate levels above the sentence such as section, chapter, and sentence cluster within a paragraph. Rather, he posits discourse, paragraph, and sentence, plus recursion, as being the three basic units necessary to any discourse (1983b: 271–72). Thus,

> Any string of paragraphs that belong together can be shown to have the structure of a discourse of a recognizable type; and . . . any string

---

New Testament discourse analysis. David Alan Black's *Linguistics for Students of New Testament Greek* (1988) is a successful nontechnical effort at dealing with the interrelations between linguistics and NT Greek grammar. Finally, Peter Cotterell and Max Turner's *Linguistics and Biblical Interpretation* (1989) is an excellent introduction to the relevance of linguistics for biblical exegesis. In addition, several journals have for some time now highlighted a discourse-oriented approach to the biblical text: *Linguistica Biblica, Neotestamentica, The Bible Translator*, and *Journal of Translation and Textlinguistics*, to name four.

3. For a discussion of tagmemics, see Davis 1973: 173–216; Longacre 1976: 1–44; and Pike 1982.

4. The most complete presentation of Longacre's approach is given in his *Grammar of Discourse* (1983b). Application of his method to biblical texts can be seen in Longacre 1979a, 1983a, 1985, and 1989. His work on biblical texts has had only limited exposure in the world of Old and New Testament studies.

of sentences that belong together can be shown to constitute a paragraph of recognizable type. . . . Thus the constituents of a discourse are discourse level slots which are filled either by a paragraph or an embedded discourse (with the latter ultimately composed of paragraphs as well). Similarly, the constituents of a paragraph are paragraph level slots which are filled by sentences or paragraphs (with the latter ultimately composed of sentences as well) (1983b: 272).

Longacre has developed a taxonomy of paragraph types to be used in the analysis of a text's constituency structure (Longacre 1979b, 1980). By "paragraph" he means a structural rather than an orthographic unit. In the analysis of Philemon below, I will attempt to segment the epistle into sentences and paragraphs and then justify the segmentation linguistically.

A second feature of texts according to Longacre is "texture," which he further defines under the two rubrics *spectrum* and *profile* (Longacre 1981, 1982). Spectrum is the term applied to the analysis of various levels of information relevance in a given discourse. A metaphor derived from optics, it suggests that a text has a clause structure revealing a cline of information that ranges from foregrounded (primary) events to backgrounded (secondary/tertiary) events (Longacre 1981: 340). It is Longacre's contention that the verb forms/clause types of any language can be hierarchically ranked in a manner relevant to the main line of development in a given text type. Hence, in narrative discourse, clauses with the simple past tense would tend to be the most salient (prominent), while the most static (backgrounded) clauses would tend to have stative verb forms ("to be," etc.). Expository discourse has a verb-rank scheme that is the inverse of narrative so that the two static forms (equative verbs, etc.) would rank the highest. Hortatory discourse would have command forms (imperatives, etc.) at the apex of the verb cline, while participial and nominal clauses would be backgrounded. In my paragraph analysis of Philemon (a piece of hortatory discourse) I will treat sentences whose main verb(s)/clause(s) are imperatives or other command forms or command surrogates as structurally dominant and those of lower rank as structurally ancillary. This main line versus ancillary ranking of clauses/sentences will likewise allow us to determine which paragraph(s) are more salient (thematic) in the epistle.

In addition to spectrum, a text also has profile, the term used to describe the development of plot or theme. A grammatical profile of a given discourse is deduced from clearly marked features in the surface structure. NT epistolary genre is marked by a well-defined opening (salutation), body, and finis (conclusion/benediction). Furthermore, since few discourses are spoken or written on a uniform level of excitation, Longacre posits the notion of "peak" as a further element in a text's profile. He defines peak as "any episode-like unit set apart by special surface structure features and corresponding to the Climax or Denouement in the notional [deep] structure" (Longacre 1983b: 24). Peak is essentially a "non-routine zone of turbulence" (1983b: xvii) in the surface structure of a discourse. Peak is marked by such features as rhetorical underlining, concentration of participants, heightened vividness (shift in the nominal/verbal balance, tense, third person to second or first, etc.), change of pace (shift to short crisp sentences/paragraphs or to a long run-on type of sentence/paragraph structure), change of vantage point and/or orientation, and so on (Longacre 1981: 349–351; 1983b: 25–38). In my analysis of Philemon it will be shown how peak is marked in the most salient paragraph of the epistle.

Finally, a text has macrostructure—the main point or theme of the discourse. This can be arrived at by the analysis of the interplay between the constituency structure and the texture (particularly the verb-rank scheme) for the particular text. In one sense, the macrostructure is logically prior to the other two features of text in that an author has in mind what he wants to communicate before he structures this information into the finished product, a spoken or written text.

Longacre's model may be illustrated by the diagram below in which the two-way arrows are to be read as "mutually supports and is mutually dependent upon":

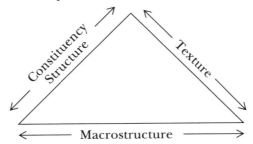

Philemon As Hortatory Discourse

The Epistle to Philemon provides a fertile field of investigation into the nature of hortatory discourse.[5] In hortatory discourse, the basic schema seems to be problem, command, motivation. In Philemon, motivation precedes problem and command. Actually, the text is long on motivation with mitigated exhortation (command surrogates) and

5. Consult Roberts 1987 for the most recent survey of work done on Philemon.

short on overt commands. This will be seen in the paragraph structure of the book, as the most salient command form (imperative) does not occur until v. 17.

Perhaps some word should be said about participant identification and the communication situation in Philemon. The letter was written by the Apostle Paul to an individual named Philemon, a Christian who lived at Colossae and who was probably led to faith in Christ through the ministry of Paul. Philemon owned a slave, Onesimus, who had run away and apparently had met Paul in Rome. There Onesimus became a Christian, and now Paul has dispatched him and this letter back to Philemon at Colossae. The purpose of the letter is to exhort Philemon to forgive Onesimus and to receive him back without retribution. Secondary participants are mentioned in the text but play no significant role.[6]

This letter provides a fascinating background for the study of sociolinguistic factors.[7] One of the most serious offenses known in the ancient world was for a slave to run away. Consider the difficulty in writing a letter in that day and time requesting pardon for a runaway slave, particularly in light of the possibility that he had been guilty of theft as well. Paul had to ask Philemon to excuse his own presumption in detaining Onesimus for so long. Furthermore, he had to avoid all appearance of dictating terms to his friend which easily could have defeated his purpose. Paul employs psychological tact while at the same time not sacrificing his apostolic authority. His method is subtle, adroit, delicate. The Book of Philemon is a classic example of the use of mitigated exhortation.

Sentence and Paragraph Segmentation

Before the text can be segmented into paragraphs, the sentences must be identified.[8] In Greek discourse this is not always an easy task. One must beware of simply accepting the sentence closure of the printed Greek text. A relative pronoun may often be functioning as the beginning of a new sentence (cf. ὅν in v. 12); Robertson 1943: 443). I propose that the text be segmented into the following twenty-two sentences:

6. For further information on the background of Philemon consult Lohse 1971 and O'Brien 1982 and their respective bibliographies.

7. For an excellent discussion of the sociological factors in Philemon, consult Petersen 1985, esp. 65–78, 89–109, 131–34, and 287–302.

8. In this analysis, I am primarily interested in the inter-sentential and inter-paragraph relations. Intra-sentential, intra-clausal, and other lower level matters are not dealt with here unless they shed light on a high-level relation. Clause, phrase, and word studies are handled quite well by the commentators.

Sentence number	Verse numbers	Sentence number	Verse numbers
1	1–2	12	17
2	3	13	18
3	4–5	14	19
4	6	15	20a
5	7	16	20b
6	8–9	17	21
7	10–11	18	22a
8	12	19	22b
9	13	20	23
10	14	21	24
11	15–16	22	25

The following is the paragraph segmentation which I posit for Philemon and will attempt to justify linguistically below:

Paragraph number	Sentence numbers	Verse numbers
1	1–2	1–3
2	3–5	4–7
3	6–11	8–16
4	12–16	17–20
5	17–19	21–22
6	20–22	23–25

The letter of Philemon fits the usual tripartite structure of NT epistles. There is an introductory salutation: paragraph 1; body: paragraphs 2–5; and closure: paragraph 6. Since both the salutation and closure are fairly fixed forms of letter writing, I will simply comment on their contribution to our understanding of the total letter without offering a diagrammed paragraph analysis of them.

Structure of the Salutation

Characteristics of opening salutations is their lack of finite verbal forms. Thus a literal reading would be "Paul, a prisoner of Christ Jesus and Timothy our brother to Philemon our beloved one and fellow-worker" (v. 1). The chief purpose of a salutation is to identify the writer, the reader, sometimes the location of the reader, and to offer greetings. It is interesting that Paul does not identify himself as an "apostle" in the salutation, perhaps due to the nature of his request. Rather, he chooses the phrase *a prisoner of Christ*. The full rhetorical and sociolinguistic implications of this choice are not apparent until the entire letter has been read (see White 1971: 35).

Since the letter is addressed to Philemon, why is there specific mention in the salutation of his family and the church which met in his house? It would appear that while Paul intended this as a personal letter, he also intended that this matter have a special message to the local church as well. Indeed, whatever Philemon's response to the return of Onesimus, the church would know, and this bit of added "pressure" may be accounted for on the basis of the sociolinguistic factors evident in the epistle. Notice the shift from the singular personal pronouns throughout the epistle to the plural use of ὑμῶν and ὑμῖν in v. 22.

The structure of the salutation appears to be an expository CO-ORDINATE paragraph[9] with two sentences of equal weight, sentence 1 (vv. 1–2) and sentence 2 (v. 3). Some form of the verb *write* is probably to be understood in sentence 1, while the optative πληθυνθείη 'let it be multiplied' would give the sense of sentence 2: "May grace and peace . . . be multiplied to you."

The body of the epistle consists of paragraphs 2–5. It has very definite boundaries which mark it off from the salutation and the closure. The use of the performative εὐχαριστῶ (v. 4) is the first occurrence of a finite verb in the letter. An expression of thanksgiving to God for the recipient is indicative of the beginning of the body of the letter. Body closure is marked by the verb ἀσπάζεταί 'to greet' at the beginning of paragraph 6, followed by the names of those sending greetings.

Structure of Paragraph 2 (vv. 4–7)

Paragraph 2 (vv. 4–7) also has definite boundaries. The performative verb εὐχαριστῶ marks paragraph onset while the vocative Ἀδελφέ at the end of v. 7 marks paragraph closure. The repetition of the notion of "love for the saints" in vv. 5 and 7 serves almost like an inclusio to give cohesion to the paragraph. Traditionally, this THANKS-GIVING paragraph has been separated from the body proper. For purposes of this analysis, however, I am considering "body" to refer to everything other than the formulaic salutation and closure.

9. Longacre posits a finite set of twenty-four semantic paragraph types, many of which are used in the analysis of Philemon. These are discussed and illustrated in Longacre 1979b, 1980, and 1983. With each type that occurs in Philemon, I will offer a brief definition from Longacre.

Table 1. Philemon 4–7 (E): REASON Paragraph

TEXT: SIMPLE PARAGRAPH

vv. 4–5 INTRODUCTION: Εὐχαριστῶ τῷ θεῷ μου πάντοτε μνείαν σου ποιούμενος ἐπὶ τῶν προσευχῶν μου ἀκούων σου τὴν ἀγάπην καὶ τὴν
πίστιν ἣν ἔχεις πρὸς τὸν κύριον Ἰησοῦν καὶ εἰς πάντας τοὺς ἁγίους.

v. 6 TEXT: ὅπως ἡ κοινωνία τῆς πίστεώς σου ἐνεργὴς γένηται ἐν ἐπι-
γνώσει παντὸς ἀγαθοῦ τοῦ ἐν ἡμῖν εἰς χριστόν.

v. 7 REASON: χαρὰν γὰρ πολλὴν ἔσχον καὶ παράκλησιν ἐπὶ τῇ ἀγάπῃ σου ὅτι
τὰ σπλάγχνα τῶν ἁγίων ἀναπέπαυται διὰ σοῦ ἀδελφέ.

I believe this paragraph (see table 1) is best described as an EX-POSITORY REASON paragraph whose TEXT[10] is composed of sentences 3–4 (vv. 4–6) and its REASON of sentence 5 (v. 7). The TEXT (vv. 4–6) it-self embeds a SIMPLE paragraph with an INTRODUCTION (vv. 4–5) and TEXT (v. 6). The INTRODUCTION (vv. 4–5) is a REASON sentence with v. 4 the main clause and the reason introduced by the participle ἀκούων in v. 5: "I give thanks . . . because I hear. . . . " Γὰρ in v. 7 introduces a sentence subordinate to the preceding two sentences because se-mantically the clause that supplies a reason is subordinate to the clause it explains.[11]

A REASON paragraph encodes efficient cause or reason for an ac-tion. A SIMPLE paragraph is one in which there is one sentence in its body but which may also contain a second sentence that initiates or terminates the paragraph (Longacre 1980: 6). Verses 4–5 serve as the INTRODUCTION to the STATEMENT of v. 6.

There is an exegetical problem in v. 6 with the conjunction ὅπως. Is it to be related to μνείαν ποιούμενος or ἣν ἔχεις, or can it be construed as the beginning of a new sentence with the main verb (προσεύχομαι) left unexpressed? I agree with Louw (1982: 118–19) that the latter of these constructions is the best option and have posited a new sentence beginning with v. 6.

Having made v. 6 the beginning of a new sentence, a reason must be offered for analyzing it as the most salient piece of information in the embedded SIMPLE paragraph (vv. 4–6). Friberg and Friberg (1981: 657) give the conjunction ὅπως a hyperordinating-conjunction tag in

10. Longacre uses the term TEXT to identify the most salient part of a paragraph, i.e., that which carries the most semantic weight. His paragraph types are identified by the semantic function of the least-weighted member. Hence, a REASON paragraph is one in which the most important information is conveyed in the TEXT portion of the sentence or embedded paragraph rather than in the REASON portion.

11. The conjunction γὰρ is always considered by Friberg and Friberg 1981: 834 (for semantic reasons) to introduce a subordinate clause/sentence in the Greek NT.

v. 6, which raises its position on the semantic scale of prominence. Traditional Greek grammar recognizes two clausal relationships: coordinate and subordinate. On the basis of semantic analysis rather than syntactical, Friberg and Friberg have added a third logical possibility: superordination. A superordinate conjunction introduces a clause that is more prominent than the one to which it is related (Friberg and Friberg 1981: 833–34). Since I have analyzed v. 6 as the beginning of a new sentence, its relationship to the previous sentence (vv. 4–5) is one of superordination because the content of the prayer is more salient than the reason for the prayer. Furthermore, it is only after we have read the entire epistle that the function of v. 6 in the overall discourse becomes clear. The content of Paul's prayer is an ever-so-mild hint of the full-blown exhortation to come in v. 17. Thus, I have analyzed this embedded SIMPLE paragraph (4–6) as INTRODUCTION (vv. 4–5) and TEXT (v. 6).

The verb structure of this paragraph further warrants describing it as basically EXPOSITORY. After the initial εὐχαριστῶ, the verb forms are mostly relational in nature and very low on the transitivity scale. This paragraph is highly descriptive of Philemon's Christian character, and thus we have verbs and verbals like "to hear," "to have" (twice), and "to become." The final verb in the paragraph is a perfect passive ("has been refreshed") that appears in a subordinate ὅτι clause. No command forms or command surrogates occur.

Paragraph 2 has both an overt and a covert function in the epistle. Since it is EXPOSITORY (containing no overt or mitigated command forms), it functions to express to Philemon the reason that Paul thanks God for his Christian behavior. This explains why there are so many TEXT-REASON relationships embedded in the sentence structure as well as in the overall paragraph. However, I believe we can surmise a further function lying behind this paragraph, a covert function. That function is to prepare Philemon for the request which Paul plans to make in v. 17. Mention is made of his love and faith toward all the saints, his fellowship of faith which leads to the knowing and doing of all that is good, and the statement that the innermost beings of the saints have been refreshed because of him. Paul's employment of σπλάγχνα in v. 7 rhetorically prepares Philemon for his request (note its use also in vv. 12 and 20). Church (1978: 24) highlights the rhetorical effectiveness of this term on Philemon by noting that "if Philemon refreshes the very hearts of the saints (v. 7); and, if Onesimus is Saint Paul's very heart (v. 12); then, to refresh Paul's very heart, Philemon must refresh Onesimus (v. 20)." Semantically, paragraph 2 serves a covert purpose of setting the stage for Paul's request.

Table 2. Philemon 8–16 (H): AMPLIFICATION Paragraph

vv. 8–9   TEXT: διὸ πολλὴν ἐν χριστῷ παρρησίαν ἔχων ἐπιτάσσειν σοι τὸ
           ἀνῆκον διὰ τὴν ἀγάπην μᾶλλον παρακαλῶ τοιοῦτος ὢν ὡς
           Παῦλος πρεσβύτης νυνὶ δὲ καὶ δέσμιος χριστοῦ Ἰησοῦ.
           AMPLIFICATION: COMMENT PARAGRAPH
              TEXT: AMPLIFICATION PARAGRAPH
vv. 10–11   TEXT: παρακαλῶ σε περὶ τοῦ ἐμοῦ τέκνου ὃν ἐγέν-
                νησα ἐν τοῖς δεσμοῖς Ὀνήσιμον τόν ποτέ σοι
                ἄχρηστον νυνὶ δὲ καὶ σοὶ καὶ ἐμοὶ εὔχρηστον.
                AMPLIFICATION: REASON PARAGRAPH
v. 12   TEXT: ὃν ἀνέπεμψά σοι αὐτόν τοῦτ᾽ ἔστιν τὰ
                  ἐμὰ σπλάγχνα.
                  REASON: ANTITHETICAL PARAGRAPH
v. 13   THESIS: ὃν ἐγὼ ἐβουλόμην πρὸς ἐμαυτὸν
                    κατέχειν ἵνα ὑπὲρ σοῦ μοι διακονῇ ἐν
                    τοῖς δεσμοῖς τοῦ εὐαγγελίου.
v. 14   ANTITHESIS: χωρὶς δὲ τῆς σῆς γνώμης
                    οὐδὲν ἠθέλησα ποιῆσαι ἵνα μὴ ὡς κατὰ
                    ἀνάγκην τὸ ἀγαθόν σου ᾖ ἀλλὰ κατὰ
                    ἑκούσιον.
vv. 15–16   COMMENT: τάχα γὰρ διὰ τοῦτο ἐχωρίσθη πρὸς ὥραν ἵνα
                αἰώνιον αὐτὸν ἀπέχῃς οὐκέτι ὡς δοῦλον ἀλλ᾽ ὑπὲρ δοῦλον
                ἀδελφὸν ἀγαπητόν μάλιστα ἐμοί πόσῳ δὲ μᾶλλον σοὶ καὶ
                ἐν σαρκὶ καὶ ἐν κυρίῳ.

Structure of Paragraph 3 (vv. 8–16)

Paragraph 3 (vv. 8–16) is a hortatory AMPLIFICATION paragraph with the mitigated command form "beseech." The following considerations led to the suggestion of the paragraph boundaries between vv. 8 and 16. First, the conjunction διό in v. 8 signals a new paragraph. The appearance of the conjunction οὖν in v. 17 marks a new paragraph at that point as well. The topic of conversation shifts in v. 8 to Onesimus and to Paul's justification to Philemon for the reasons that Onesimus should be received again as a Christian brother. Finally, there is an inclusio formed by the phrase ἐν χριστῷ at the beginning of v. 8 and the phrase ἐν κυρίῳ at the end of v. 16. This phrase does not occur anywhere else within this paragraph.

I take this paragraph to be a hortatory AMPLIFICATION paragraph whose TEXT consists of vv. 8–9 and an AMPLIFICATION in vv. 10–16 (see table 2). The amplification portion of the paragraph reflects multiple levels of embedding. For example, the AMPLIFICATION paragraph (vv. 10–16) embeds a COMMENT paragraph whose TEXT is vv. 10–14 and COMMENT vv. 15–16. The TEXT of that COMMENT paragraph also embeds

an AMPLIFICATION paragraph whose TEXT is vv. 10–11 and AMPLIFICATION
vv. 12–14. This AMPLIFICATION paragraph further embeds a REASON
paragraph whose TEXT is v. 12 and REASON vv. 13–14. Finally, the
REASON paragraph embeds an ANTITHETICAL paragraph with THESIS
(v. 13) and ANTITHESIS (v. 14).

Four paragraph types are identified in this large paragraph: AMPLI-
FICATION, COMMENT, REASON, and ANTITHETICAL. AMPLIFICATION and COMMENT
paragraphs fall under the general head of EMBELLISHMENT paragraphs
according to Longacre (1980: 14). The AMPLIFICATION paragraph employs a set of two or more sentences to develop a theme by bringing in
additional information in each successive sentence. The result is a
"circling-in-on-the-target" type structure. Notice how vv. 10–11 further amplify vv. 8–9. The COMMENT paragraph involves the speaker or
writer in some personal observation of his own (Longacre 1980: 16).
Notice how vv. 15–16 function in this way. The REASON paragraph has
been discussed above. The ANTITHETICAL paragraph encodes contrast,
frustration, or expectancy reversal (Longacre 1980: 10). This is
marked among other ways in the surface structure of Greek by the use
of δὲ as in v. 14. Paul desired to keep Onesimus with him, but he would
not do so without Philemon's consent. Notice that semantically v. 14
is a further explication of ἀνέπεμψά in v. 12, so that v. 14 furnishes the
ANTITHESIS to v. 13, and together the two function as the REASON for the
statement of v. 12.

This is the most involuted paragraph of the book in terms of
structure. Paul is not yet ready to command, but he uses some clear
command surrogates which extenuate exhortation to Philemon.
Paul informs Philemon at the outset that he has a specific request to
make of him, but the content of the request is deferred until a bit
later. In vv. 10–16, Paul gradually clarifies the content of his request. The structure of this paragraph reflects the very reserved way
in which Paul approaches Philemon with his request. Almost every
statement is a further AMPLIFICATION on the preceding statement: I
beseech you . . . I beseech you for Onesimus . . . I beseech you for
Onesimus whom I have begotten in my bonds. . . . The result of this
kind of structure gives the impression of "circling in on the target."
Furthermore, the verb which Paul chooses for receiving Onesimus
(ἀπέχῃς) is in the subjunctive mood, the mood of potentiality, and
this is the only subjunctive in the entire paragraph (the only other
one in the book up to this point is γένηται in v. 6).

The sociolinguistic relationships in this paragraph become quite
interesting upon study. Up to this point, Paul has not made any
effort to remind Philemon of his authority as an apostle or to com-

mand him on the basis of that authority. However, all of this changes in vv. 8–9 as Paul says: "Wherefore, although I have much boldness in Christ to charge you [to do] that which is fitting, yet because of love, I rather beseech, being such a one as Paul, an old man and now also a prisoner of Christ Jesus." Here we see Paul pulling rank on Philemon, although in a very mitigated fashion. He informs Philemon that although he could charge him to do the right thing, yet he chooses rather for love's sake to beseech or encourage him to do what is right. Both the infinitive ἐπιτάσσειν 'to charge' and the main verb παρακαλῶ 'I beseech' are examples of mitigated command. Paul must get Philemon's attention but yet not come on too strong too soon. Notice the preposed διὰ τὴν ἀγάπην in v. 9 (before the verb παρακαλῶ, which gives emphasis to "love" and deemphasizes the exhortation. Through the repetition of the verb παρακαλῶ in v. 10 "Paul pulls Philemon's heartstrings not once, but twice" (Church 1978: 26). Note that Onesimus is not mentioned until the end of the clause (v. 10). Thus, a literal rendering would be: "I beseech you concerning my own son, whom I have begotten in my bonds, Onesimus."

Wickert interprets the participle ὤν in v. 9 as a concessive participle and thus begins a new sentence at v. 9b: "Although I am none other than Paul . . . I beseech." In this way vv. 8–9a are rhetorically balanced with vv. 9b–10 by means of tautological parallelism (Wickert 1961: 235). However, it seems best, following Lightfoot, to take τοιοῦτος ὤν with the preceding sentence and construe the resumptive παρακαλῶ as the beginning of a new sentence (Lightfoot 1959: 338).

Paul continues in v. 11 with a comment about the profitableness of Onesimus to both himself and Philemon. Onesimus's name means "profitable"—hence the play on words which Paul employs in v. 11. Verse 12 states the fact of Paul's having sent Onesimus back to Philemon, and perhaps there the verb *receive* is to be supplied in the context. The text reads: "Whom I have sent to you, him, that is my own heart." We may have here a case of mitigation through ellipsis. Paul is not yet ready to command Philemon as he does in v. 17. It is also possible that no verb is to be supplied, and Paul simply further identifies Onesimus through a somewhat broken construction as "him, that is my own heart."

Verse 13 may be interpreted as a covert request on Paul's part that Philemon allow Onesimus to remain with him as his assistant in the gospel. Paul does not overtly request this, but he does mention the fact of his own intent to this effect. Paul did not presume upon Philemon's generosity in this area and thus sent Onesimus back to him. Note the statement in v. 14, "but without your opinion I was

Table 3. Philemon 17–20 (H): PARAPHRASE Paragraph

TEXT: COMMENT PARAGRAPH
    TEXT: SIMPLE PARAGRAPH
v. 17   TEXT: εἰ οὖν με ἔχεις κοινωνόν, προσλαβοῦ αὐτὸν ὡς ἐμέ.
    COMMENT: REASON PARAGRAPH
v. 18   TEXT: εἰ δέ τι ἠδίκησέν σε ἢ ὀφείλει, τοῦτο ἐμοὶ ἐλλόγα.
v. 19   REASON: ἐγὼ Παῦλος ἔγραψα τῇ ἐμῇ χειρί, ἐγὼ ἀποτίσω ἵνα μὴ
               λέγω σοι ὅτι καὶ σεαυτόν μοι προσοφείλεις.
PARAPHRASE: PARAPHRASE PARAGRAPH
v. 20   PARAPHRASE: ναί ἀδελφέ, ἐγώ σου ὀναίμην ἐν κυρίῳ
        TEXT: ἀνάπαυσόν μου τὰ σπλάγχνα ἐν Χριστῷ.

willing to do nothing, in order that not as by way of necessity the good of you might be, but rather by way of [being] voluntary." How cleverly Paul inserts this idea, perhaps with the intent that Philemon will agree not only to forgive Onesimus and receive him back, but even more, may free him completely to serve alongside of Paul.

Thus, the clause structure of this paragraph again reveals no overt imperatives. Nevertheless, by means of skillful use of mitigation, Paul covertly begins to apply the pressure in preparation for the overt command about to be definitized in v. 17.

Structure of Paragraph 4 (vv. 17–20)

Verses 17–20 constitute the fourth major paragraph and what I consider to be the PEAK of the book. I take this to be a hortatory PARAPHRASE paragraph, which further embeds a SIMPLE, COMMENT, and REASON paragraph, whose TEXT is v. 17, containing the most salient verb in the epistle: προσλαβοῦ.

SIMPLE, COMMENT, and REASON paragraph types have been defined above. The PARAPHRASE paragraph states the same thing in a different way. It can have a generic-specific type of structure in which sentence 1 would give the general information while sentences 2–N would give details, or vice versa where sentences 1, 2, and following would encode the details and sentence N would give a summary (Longacre 1980: 14–15).

In Philemon 17–20, vv. 17–19 compose the TEXT while v. 20 gives a PARAPHRASE of the text (see table 3). The TEXT embeds a COMMENT paragraph whose TEXT is v. 17 and COMMENT vv. 18–19. This COMMENT paragraph further embeds a SIMPLE paragraph with v. 17 as the TEXT. This paragraph (composed of a single sentence) contains the most salient verb in the epistle and provides a concise statement of the

macrostructure of Philemon: "Receive him as you would receive me."
The COMMENT paragraph further embeds a REASON paragraph whose
TEXT is v. 18 and REASON v. 19. This paragraph informs Philemon that
he can charge anything to Paul's account because he has written it
with his own hand and will repay any debt. Finally, v. 20 contains a
PARAPHRASE paragraph with the most salient verb being the imperative
ἀνάπαυσόν 'refresh', and thus it is tagged as the TEXT.

This paragraph is clearly marked in the surface structure by the
use of οὖν in v. 17. There is a shift at v. 17 from the indicative mode
to the imperative mood, and then v. 21 shifts back to the indicative.

The following surface-structure features mark this paragraph as
the PEAK of the book. First, there is a definite shift in the verb structure. Up until this point, there has been no imperative used. However, here at the PEAK of the book and within the confines of only four
verses, three command forms appear. The most salient of the three
appears in v. 17 and gives a unique summary of the book: "Receive
him [Onesimus] as you would receive me." Furthermore, there are
no less than eleven verbs in this paragraph, and not one of them is a
verbal (participle or infinitive). In the preceding paragraph of eight
verses there are only seventeen verb forms, and five of those are verbals. There is a wide range of mode shift in these four verses as well,
including the use of the imperative, indicative, and optative modes.

The sentence structure of this paragraph is different from the
preceding material in that Paul shifts to short, almost staccato, sentences with very few preposed and postposed clauses. This added
"punch" is further magnified by the increase in finite verb forms.
All of these features combine to mark vv. 17–20 as the peak of
the book.

In this paragraph all the stops are pulled out, in that Paul is
overtly "twisting the arm" of Philemon to comply with his command.
The sociolinguistic factor of mitigation seen in the previous paragraphs is all but abandoned here as blunt imperatives occur. Furthermore, Paul reminds Philemon how he owes even his own being
(probably a reference to his salvation) to Paul. The structure at this
point is interesting. The clause ἵνα μὴ λέγω has an imperatival sense,
though it is not a surface-structure imperative. It is actually embedded in a postposed sentence margin following the independent
clause *I will repay*. Thus Paul employs a further argument for
Philemon to receive Onesimus back.

The only example of the first-person optative to express a wish in
the NT occurs in v. 20: ὀναίμην 'let me benefit'. This in turn is followed
by a final independent clause with an overt imperative ἀνάπαυσόν

Table 4. Philemon 21–22 (H):
SIMULTANEOUS Paragraph (Closure of body)

v. 21   SIMULTANEOUS 1: πεποιθὼς τῇ ὑπακοῇ σου ἔγραψά σοι εἰδὼς ὅτι καὶ
         ὑπὲρ ἃ λέγω ποιήσεις.
v. 22   SIMULTANEOUS 2: ἅμα δὲ καὶ ἑτοίμαζέ μοι ξενίαν ἐλπίζω γὰρ ὅτι διὰ τῶν
         προσευχῶν ὑμῶν χαρισθήσομαι ὑμῖν.

'refresh', harking back to what was stated in v. 7. Thus Paul is found to
play notes all up and down the scale of verb salience for hortatory
Greek discourse in an effort to sway Philemon to accept Onesimus.

Structure of Paragraph 5 (vv. 21–22)

The final paragraph to be studied is found in vv. 21–22 (see table 4).
I take it to be a hortatory SIMULTANEOUS paragraph with a covert command form in the first sentence and an overt imperative in the second (see table 4). There is a certain balance between the two
sentences that is further shown by the use of the coordinating conjunction δὲ at the beginning of v. 22.

Under the heading of "temporal paragraphs," Longacre posits two
types: those that encode chronological sequence and those that encode simultaneity or overlap (Longacre 1980: 8–9). In English, overlap
may be marked in the surface structure by "meanwhile," "at the same
time," or a preposed adverbial clause introduced by "as." Philemon 22
is introduced by the adverbial ἅμα 'at the same time' which is the
surface-structure device that here encodes the notion of temporal
overlap. Paul's thought may be summarized as "I have written knowing
that you will do beyond what I have asked [namely, receive Onesimus
back], and at the same time [of your receiving Onesimus] prepare a
place for my lodging [prepare to receive me as well]."

The paragraph boundary between vv. 20–21 is not as clear as
other places and has led some to consider v. 21 as part of the preceding paragraph. Its relation to that paragraph would then be some
sort of summary statement. While I agree it is a summation, I do not
believe this to be an accurate way of analyzing the text for the following reasons. There is not a single nonfinite verb form in vv. 17–20,
yet v. 21 begins with the participle πεποιθὼς. This does not mean, of
course, that v. 21 could not go with the preceding paragraph, only
that in my opinion it is more likely that it does not. Furthermore, the
scope of the ἔγραψά in v. 21 harks back, not only to the command of
the preceding paragraph, but also to the entire epistle up to this
point. Such summation probably merits a new paragraph.

The only overt imperative in this paragraph is found in v. 22, in which Paul asks Philemon to prepare lodging for him. This imperative is clearly not of the same nature as the preceding three, and thus without question we are in a new paragraph by v. 22. However, there is a covert command in v. 21 embedded in the postposed ὅτι clause. After the salvo of imperatives in the preceding paragraph, there is no need for Paul to continue the appeal with another imperative. Rather, he in effect mitigates a command by saying, "I know that you will do beyond what I have asked." Although the main verb in this sentence is the performative ἔγραψά, it does not convey the most prominent information. In the case of v. 21, what is grammatically subordinate (the ὅτι clause) is semantically prominent. The same kind of thing occurs in 1 John 2:1–6, where v. 1a reads ταῦτα γράφω ὑμῖν ἵνα μὴ ἁμάρτητε. Longacre identifies this as a hortatory REASON paragraph whose TEXT is vv. 1–2 and REASON vv. 3–6. He notes that the REASON portion of the paragraph goes with μὴ ἁμάρτητε rather than the ταῦτα γράφω. The sense of the paragraph is "don't sin, because. . . . " The command element is expressed in a postposed ἵνα clause, but it semantically dominates the paragraph (Longacre 1983a: 9). Hence, 1 John 2:1–6 is hortatory, though it appears upon first blush to be purely expository.

Thus Philemon 21–22 is a hortatory SIMULTANEOUS paragraph which functions as closure for the main body of the epistle by summarizing again Paul's request via mitigation and adding an additional request to prepare lodging for an impending visit by the apostle.

Final greetings are expressed in vv. 23–25, and, due to their formulaic nature, they need not detain us here. Paul appends a list of the names of people who are apparently with him at the time of writing and who send their greetings to Philemon. The closing sentence of this paragraph expresses the usual benediction of grace.

Macrostructure, Constituent Structure, and Texture of Philemon

We are now ready to deduce an overall macrostructure for Philemon based on the above analysis. Excluding the salutation and finis which open and close the epistle in a formal manner, paragraph 2 (vv. 4–7) semantically functions as what we might call grounds 1, while paragraph 3 (vv. 8–16) semantically functions as grounds 2 for the (thematic and most salient) exhortation of paragraph 4 (vv. 17–20). The most salient clause of paragraph 4 (and of the entire epistle) is v. 17. Paragraph 5 (vv. 21–22) summarizes and mitigates the exhortation of

paragraph 4, makes a secondary request to prepare lodging, and
serves as closure for the main body of the epistle. Thus, from the
most-prominent clause in the epistle according to my analysis the
following macrostructure can be deduced: "Receive Onesimus as you
would receive me."

The "constituent structure" of Philemon contains twenty-two sentences which comprise six paragraphs. Paragraphs 1 and 6 comprise
the salutation and closure and have not been analyzed in this study.
The middle four paragraphs (body) exhibit multiple layers of embedding and reveal the hierarchical structure of Philemon. Second, the
"texture" of Philemon reveals the development of theme and shows
how the verb scheme of Philemon fits that of hortatory discourse. The
PEAK of this epistle is vv. 17–20, with v. 17 containing the most salient
clause in the entire piece. This information yields a viable macrostructure for the text.

The interfusion of discourse analysis with traditional exegesis
serves to explicate the meaning of Philemon so that we are allowed
to account for the textual features in a more thorough and holistic
way. The result of my analysis shows the epistle to be a carefully written document which reflects Paul's rhetorical art in handling a delicate situation. The Epistle to Philemon is a beautiful piece of
mitigated arm-twisting!

References

de Beaugrande, R., and J. W. Dressler
    1981   *Introduction to Text Linguistics.* London: Longmans.
Beekman, John, and John Callow
    1974   *Translating the Word of God.* Grand Rapids: Zondervan.
Beekman, John, John Callow, and M. Kopesec
    1981   *The Semantic Structure of Written Communication.* Dallas: Summer
            Institute of Linguistics.
Black, David Alan
    1988   *Linguistics for Students of New Testament Greek: A Survey of Basic
            Concepts and Applications.* Grand Rapids: Baker.
    1992   *Linguistics and New Testament Interpretation: Essays on Discourse
            Analysis.* Nashville: Broadman
Church, F. F.
    1978   "Rhetorical Structure and Design in Paul's Letter to Philemon."
            Harvard Theological Review 71:17–33.

Cotterell, Peter, and Max Turner
  1989   *Linguistics and Biblical Interpretation*. Downers Grove, Illinois: InterVarsity.
Davis, Philip W.
  1973   *Modern Theories of Language*. Englewood Cliffs, New Jersey: Prentice Hall.
Erickson, Richard J.
  1983   "Linguistics and Biblical Language: A Wide-open Field." *Journal of the Evangelical Theological Society* 26:257–63.
Friberg, Barbara, and Timothy Friberg
  1981   *Analytical Greek New Testament*. Grand Rapids: Baker.
Lightfoot, J. B.
  1959   *Saint Paul's Epistles to the Colossians and to Philemon*. Grand Rapids: Zondervan.
Lohse, Eduard
  1971   *Colossians and Philemon*. Translated by William R. Poehlmann and Robert J. Karris. Hermeneia. Philadelphia: Fortress.
Longacre, Robert E.
  1968   *Discourse, Paragraph, and Sentence Structure in Selected Philippine Languages*. 2 vols. Summer Institute of Linguistics Publication 11. Santa Ana: Summer Institute of Linguistics.
  1976   "Discourse." Pp. 1–44 in *Tagmemics* I: *Aspects of the field*. Edited by Ruth Brend and Kenneth Pike. Trends in Linguistics, Studies and Monographs 1. The Hague: Mouton.
  1979a   "The Discourse Structure of the Flood Narrative." *Journal of the American Academy of Religion* 47, Supplement B: 89–133.
  1979b   "The Paragraph as a Grammatical Unit." Pp. 115–34 in *Discourse and Syntax*. Edited by Talmy Givón. *Syntax and Semantics 12*. New York: Academic Press.
  1980   *An Apparatus for the Identification of Paragraph Types*. Notes on Linguistics 15. Dallas: Summer Institute of Linguistics.
  1981   "A Spectrum and Profile Approach to Discourse Analysis." *Text* 1:332–59.
  1982   "Verb Ranking and the Constituent Structure of Discourse." *Journal of the Linguistics Association of the Southwest* 5:177–202.
  1983a. *Exhortation and Mitigation in the Greek Text of the First Epistle to John*. Selected Technical Articles Related to Translation 9. Dallas: Summer Institute of Linguistics.
  1983b   *The Grammar of Discourse*. New York: Plenum.
  1985   "Interpreting Biblical Stories." Pp. 169–85 in *Discourse and Literature*. Edited by T. van Dijk. Critical Theory Series 3. Amsterdam/Philadelphia: John Benjamins.
  1989   *Joseph: A Story of Divine Providence: A Text Theoretical and Textlinguistic Analysis of Genesis 37 and 39–48*. Winona Lake, Indiana: Eisenbrauns.

In Press   Two Hypotheses Regarding Text Generation and Analysis.

Louw, J. P.

1982   *Semantics of New Testament Greek.* Atlanta: Scholars Press.

Nida, E. A., J. P. Louw, A. H. Snyman, and J. v. W. Cronje

1983   *Style and Discourse.* Cape Town, South Africa: Bible Society of South Africa.

O'Brien, Peter T.

1982   *Colossians and Philemon.* Word Biblical Commentary 44. Waco: Word.

Petersen, Norman R.

1985   *Rediscovering Paul.* Philadelphia: Fortress.

Pickering, Wilbur

1978   *A Framework for Discourse Analysis.* Dallas: Summer Institute of Linguistics.

Pike, Kenneth

1982   *Linguistic Concepts: An Introduction to Tagmemics.* Lincoln: University of Nebraska Press.

Roberts, J. H.

1987   "Filemon in Diskussie: Enkele Hoogtepunte in die Sand van Sake ("Philemon in Discussion: Some High Points in the State of Research"). *Scriptura* 21:24–50.

Robertson, A. T.

1934   *A Grammar of the Greek New Testament in the Light of Historical Research.* 4th ed. Nashville: Broadman.

White, John L.

1971   "The Structural Analysis of Philemon: A Point of Departure in the Formal Analysis of the Pauline Letter." Vol 1: pp. 1–47 in *Society of Biblical Literature Seminar Papers.* N.P.: Scholars Press.

Wickert, U.

1961   "Der Philemonbrief—Privatbrief oder apostolisches Schreiben?" *Zeitschrift für die neutestamentliche Wissenschaft* 52:230–38.

Hebrews 9:11-12: Christ's Body, Heavenly Region, or . . . ?

Sakae Kubo

Chico, California

The main thrust of Heb 9:11–12 is clear. It states that Christ entered τὰ ἅγια, not through animal blood but through his own blood. If we should omit the phrase διὰ τῆς μείζονος καὶ τελειοτέρας σκηνῆς οὐ χειροποιήτου, τοῦτ᾽ ἔστιν οὐ ταύτης τῆς κτίσεως and change the next οὐδέ to οὐ, the sentence would be perfectly understandable. However, it is because of these additional words that so much has been written about this passage.

Almost all commentators take the phrase *through the greater and more perfect tent* in connection with the main verb *entered*.[1] However, if this is the case, what does "Christ entered through the greater and

---

1. Wickham (1910: 67) connects it with the participle: "His service and the blessing which it wins have *as their sphere* the greater Tabernacle." Dods (1956: 332) follows the same view: "It was because He was High Priest not in the earthly but the heavenly tabernacle that He was able to secure these great results. . . . Christ is represented here as the High Priest ministering in the tabernacle, not passing through it." This view does not closely connect the idea with the main clause. How is the idea that the sphere is the greater tabernacle connected with his entrance into τὰ ἅγια?

more perfect tent" mean? By connecting this passage with 10:20, some interpret the phrase as referring to the body of Christ in some sense.[2] Others would connect this passage with 4:14 and 7:26 and interpret it to mean a heavenly region.

Franz Laub has one version of the first view. In interpreting this passage, he first refers to 10:20, where the veil is identified with the flesh of Jesus. Assuming that the author of Hebrews is consistent in his view of the high priestly ministry of Christ, Laub rejects the spatial view that makes the greater and more perfect tent a heavenly region where angels dwell. This passage, like that in 10:20, must have christological and soteriological significance and not be dealing with heavenly topography. Since Christ passes through the curtain in 10:20 and through the greater and and more perfect tent in 9:11 in order to enter the most holy place, Laub maintains that they cannot be distinguished from one another. Furthermore, there is a striking parallel between 10:19 (−20) and 9:11–12. In 10:19 blood and curtain (= flesh) are parallel expressions which interpret the crucifixion in its significance as access to God. In 9:11–12 the expressions *through the greater and more perfect tent* and *through his own blood* are parallel expressions which interpret the means by which Christ opened the new and abiding way mentioned in 10:20. The latter are not to be understood as a series of new elements, but as two equal elements in parallelism, so that the tent symbol of v. 11 is explained more precisely with the expression *through his own blood* of v. 12. That is, "the tent" (= his flesh) is explained as "his blood," which Laub (1980: 186–200) says stands for the crucifixion or (more exactly) as the salvific significance of the crucifixion.

Norman Young (1980–81: 204–5) also takes this approach when he says that "the greater and more perfect tent" is a symbol of "the eschatologically new cultic means of access. . . . " He (1980–81: 205) further defines it as "the new covenant arrangement by which sin is radically purged and access to God is made universally available." This means that it symbolizes the sacrifice of Jesus rather than the animal sacrifices. Young (1980–81: 203–4) states that "'the greater and more perfect tent' contrasts with the total structure mentioned

2. The view that the "greater and more perfect tent" refers to the body of Christ has long standing, having been the position of such patristic authors as Chrysostom, Theodoret, Primasius, Theophylact, and Oecumenius. Other proponents include Aquinas, Bengel, and Owen. See Hughes 1977: 283–90 and Vanhoye 1965, not only for references to these proponents but also for excellent surveys of views concerning this difficult passage. Young (1980–81) also presents and critiques various views on this passage. There are different variations of this view, as the following discussion will show.

in 9:1; there is no distinction to parts implied." But surely the earlier structure in itself does not represent sacrifices, which are described later in vv. 7 and 9 and contrasted to the blood of Christ mentioned in v. 12. If the "greater and more perfect tent" contrasts with the earthly tent of v. 1, then it can only refer to the heavenly sanctuary and is in fact synonymous with τὰ ἅγια. Young (1980–81: 199) shows that the δεύτερα σκηνή is the same as τὰ ἅγια. In that case, "the greater and more perfect σκηνή" can only refer to the δεύτερα σκηνή.

To establish this point Hughes refers to 9:24, which states οὐ γὰρ εἰς χειροποίητα εἰσῆλθεν ἅγια but into heaven itself. Hughes (1977: 289–90) points out that the sanctuary into which Christ

> entered [is] defined by precisely the same terms that are used to define the *tent* in 8:2 and 9:11, namely, *true* and *not made with hands*. This linguistic correspondence shows in a striking manner that the "sanctuary" and the "tent" are the same thing. In 8:2 our author declares that Christ our High Priest is now "in heaven," where he ministers "in the sanctuary which is the true tent," and in 9:11ff. that he entered into the heavenly holy of holies through his entry into "the greater and more perfect tent."

It is difficult, therefore, to change the meaning of "the sanctuary into which Christ entered" to the sacrifice of Jesus.

Several questions arise with this interpretation. The phrase *the greater and more perfect tent* is followed by οὐ χειροποιήτου, τοῦτ' ἔστιν οὐ ταύτης τῆς κτίσεως. How is the body of Christ to be understood by this description? In what way was his body "not of this creation"? Was his body other than human? The other question is how is this to be understood in the light of Heb 8:2, where τὰ ἅγια and ἡ σκηνὴ ἡ ἀληθινή seem to be identical and also clearly distinguished from Christ? He is τῶν ἁγίων λειτουργὸς καὶ τῆς σκηνῆς τῆς ἀληθινῆς.

Commentators refer to the fact that there is a contrast made between the earthly sanctuary of 9:1–10 and the heavenly sanctuary of 9:11–22. Δέ in 9:11 corresponds to the μέν in 9:1, indicating the contrast between the old and new services: "The author focuses on the earthly pole of the earth–heaven antithesis" in 9:1–10 (Attridge 1986: 6). References to "the present time" (9:9) versus the "time of correction" (9:10), the many and the one sacrifice (9:7), external versus internal (9:9–10), point to the same antithesis. Verses 11–14, on the other hand, present "a mirror image of the preceding, focusing on the heavenly pole of the basic antithesis" (Attridge 1986: 6). The same antithesis is seen in the next section.

Thompson (1982: 106) further emphasizes this contrast:

Μείζονος and τελειοτέρας in 9:11 are used in contrast to κοσμικός in 9:1, and are reminiscent of the author's frequent use of κρείττων for the superiority of the work of Christ. The "greater and more perfect tent" of 9:11 is equivalent to the "true tent which the Lord made" in 8:2 and to the "true" sanctuary of 9:24. It is "greater and more perfect" because it is not material, as the contrast to κοσμικός in 9:1 suggests. The sanctuary of Christ, according to 9:24, is "heaven itself."

That the "greater and more perfect tent" is metaphysically superior to the old tent is further demonstrated by the negative phrase οὐ χειροποίητου, οὐ ταύτης τῆς κτίσεως. The earthly sanctuary is characterized as "hand made" in 9:11 and 9:23, and as "man-made" in 8:2. Χειροποίητος, which is parallel to κοσμικός in 9:1, has a pejorative connotation throughout Jewish literature.

On the basis of these types of comparison/contrast, Hofius (1972: 106) concludes that "the greater and more perfect tent" cannot refer to the body of Christ but must refer to the heavenly sanctuary.

Further, this σκηνή is described in 8:2 as one which *the Lord* pitched, not mortals. This description seems to be very close to that found in 9:11–12, "not made with hands." Thus both 8:2 and 9:11–12 refer to the heavenly sanctuary. It cannot then refer to the body of Christ. The phrase *the greater and more perfect tent not made with hands, not of this creation* of 9:11–12 appears to refer to τὰ ἄγια and ἡ σκηνὴ ἡ ἀληθινή 'which the Lord pitched and not man' of 8:2.

Vanhoye (1965: 22) tries to meet this objection that "the greater and more perfect tent" is "not made with hands, not of this creation" by interpreting "the greater and more perfect tent" not as the incarnate body but as the resurrected body of Christ, the temple rebuilt in three days. He alludes to Mark 14:58: "We heard him say, 'I will destroy this temple that is made with hands.'" Here the distinction "made with hands" (χειροποίητος) and "not made with hands" (ἀχειροποίητος) is set forth. Christ could not come before the Father in his incarnate condition, for flesh and blood cannot inherit the kingdom of God (1 Cor 15:50). Thus he needed a "more perfect tent" in order to enter the sanctuary (Vanhoye 1965: 24). The objection to this view is that it does not take sufficiently into consideration the context of this passage. The obvious comparison in Hebrews is to the earthly tabernacle. The idea of Christ's body as tent is not in view at all in Hebrews.[3]

---

3. David Peterson (1982: 142) points out the inappropriateness of Vanhoye's emphasis on the significance of the resurrection of Christ in the soteriology of Hebrews and the fact that the real focus in Hebrews is on Christ's death and ascension.

James Swetnam (1966: 171) interprets "the greater and more perfect tent" as the Eucharistic body of Christ, based on what appears to be inadequate evidence. He (1966: 170) sees the "food and drinks and cleansings" of v. 10 as "OT foreshadowings of the NT Eucharistic elements and baptism" and the τὰ ἅγια of v. 12 as "the holy things, i.e., cultic realities of the OT/NT dispensation." The first tent is the Eucharist as sacrifice, and the second tent is the Eucharist as food and drink. Christ's entrance into the second tent is that his entrance into the cultic realities of the Christian dispensation. The objections to this view would be numerous. Can τὰ ἅγια be used for anything else except the holy of holies in this particular context in Hebrews, especially since it is used that way throughout the epistle?[4] The conclusion that Eucharist as sacrifice refers to the "greater and more perfect tent" is highly problematic. The distinction made between the first tent and the second tent, that is, Eucharist as sacrifice and Eucharist as food and drink, is difficult to see. Nothing in the context would lead one to interpret "enters" in the sense of entering into the cultic realities.[5]

Westcott (1955: 258) interprets "the greater and more perfect tent" as Christ's body, but this body is his glorified Church, "the union of the redeemed and perfected hosts." Διά is understood as "through," not in the local sense, but in the sense of describing "that which Christ used in His work." The objection to this view is that it does not make precise the relationship of this phrase with the main verb in the clause, "he entered into the ἅγια." Thus Hughes's criticism (1977: 287) is on target when he says, "There is no way in which one can speak of his having entered into the heavenly sanctuary through the church: the church is not the means of his entry

4. It is obvious that Ἅγια refers to the holy place and Ἅγια Ἁγίων in 9:2 to the most holy place. However, because the references in 8:2; 9:8, 12, 24, 25; 10:19; 13:11 are to the high priest's activity, to the once-a-year-only Day of Atonement entrance of the high priest, τὰ ἅγια must refer to the most holy place. In addition to this, because the idea that the holy place has a pejorative connotation implying that a curtain still stands as a barrier between God and humans and therefore that access to God is not possible, τὰ ἅγια in these references can only refer to a sanctuary that is undivided, i.e., a place representing essentially the basic idea of the most holy place, whether it is named more generally the sanctuary or more specifically the most holy place. See also Young 1980–81: 198–99, who affirms that there is "incontrovertible indication" in the passages where it is used that τὰ ἅγια refers to the most holy place.

5. Williamson (1974–75: 305) affirms that there is no evidence in Hebrews that "the greater and more perfect tent" is "the Eucharistic body of Christ." He rejects Swetnam's identification of the blood of 9:12 as the "Eucharistic blood," equating it rather to Christ's sacrificial death on the cross. He calls Swetnam's attempt to find reference to the "Eucharistic body of Christ" in 9:11 "an unconvincing *tour de force.*"

into the heavenly sanctuary, but, to the contrary, he is the means of the church's entry."

This view that "the greater and more perfect tent" refers to Christ's body, whether viewed as his incarnate or resurrection/ Eucharistic/glorified body, has some serious objections.[6] Because there is strong evidence that "the greater and more perfect tent" must refer to the heavenly sanctuary, some have sought to interpret this phrase as referring to the heavenly holy place, the first σκηνή of heaven which corresponds to the first σκηνή of the earthly sanctuary. In other words, the heavenly sanctuary is thought of as corresponding to the earthly, with a first and second σκηνή.

If "the greater and more perfect tent" refers to the heavenly holy of holies, it is difficult to understand the passage since the author says that διὰ τῆς μείζονος καὶ τελειοτέρας σκηνῆς he entered the most holy. How could he enter the most holy through the greater and more perfect tent? Because of this difficulty some have resorted to the idea that the author conceives of two parts to the sanctuary corresponding to the earthly tabernacle: the holy and the most holy parts.

According to this view, διά is interpreted in the local sense and a distinction is made between "the greater and more perfect tent" and the ἅγια.[7] Some, without further elaboration, refer to this tent as that which Christ passed through after his resurrection, while others delimit it further. To them it is not the starry heaven or visible heaven but the place where angels dwell, while the most holy place is where God dwells. Christ passed through the greater and more perfect tent in order to enter the ἅγια. Some see a reference to this in Heb 4:14. This view appears to be the simplest solution to the problem and it therefore has an advantage over the others. However, a serious objection to this view is that it goes against the leading motif of the theology of the epistle by proposing that the heavenly counterpart of the earthly sanctuary includes the holy place. According to 9:6–9, access to the most holy place is possible only once a year by the high priest alone. The regular priests enter the holy place continually to fulfill their duties, but the people have no access here, much less access into the most holy

6. Schierse (1955: 56–59; 1969: 56) interprets "the greater and more perfect tent" as the entire historical existence of Christ. Loader (1981: 166) includes the following as proponents of this view: Cody, Ungeheuer, Winter, and Smith.

7. Those who take this approach include Andriessen 1971: 83–85; Delitzsch 1871: 2.80–81; Galling 1950–51; Héring 1970: 76–77; Koester 1962: 309–10; Michaelis 1971: 376–77; Michel 1966: 311–12; Moffatt 1924: 120–21; Nissilä 1979: 181–83; Peterson 1982: 143–44; Spicq 1952–53: 2.258; Weiss 1888: 220.

place.[8] And the fact that it is only once and by a single person that the most holy place is entered shows in effect that the way into the most holy place is still not open. In the Book of Hebrews, access into the most holy place becomes possible only when the blood of Christ purifies the sins of humankind, bringing complete forgiveness so that there is no more consciousness of sin. Access into the most holy place implies that sin has been disposed of and reconciliation between humans and God has taken place. Thus the holy place signifies lack of access into the presence of God because sins are not yet forgiven, and thus reconciliation has not taken place. The goal of Christ's ministry has been to remove the barrier of sin that exists between humankind and God. This barrier is represented by the curtain that hangs between the holy place and the most holy place. In fact, the author seems to imply that the first tent or holy place is a symbol for the time in which gifts and sacrifices were offered which could not perfect the conscience of the worshiper (Heb 9:8–9). The first tent, then, stood for inaccessibility to the presence of God, for a time when sins were not effectively forgiven, when one's consciousness of sin still remained because Christ's sacrifice had not taken place. To speak of a holy place in heaven would completely contradict this theology (see Young 1980–81: 198–204).

This interpretation then contradicts the central thesis of the book and, therefore, while it seems to be the most simple and logical explanation of the passage, it must be rejected.

Because of the problems of this last view some commentators take the first διά in a local sense but identify "the greater and more perfect tent" with τὰ ἅγια.[9] Since the curtain that prohibits access to God is no more, "the greater and more perfect tent" is the heavenly sanctuary, heaven itself, where God's presence is.

Hughes (1977: 290) presents weighty arguments for identifying "the greater and more perfect tabernacle" as the heavenly holy of holies, but he does not show the phrase's syntactical relationship in the sentence. He makes this somewhat puzzling statement:

> He entered into the heavenly holy of holies through his entry into "the greater and more perfect tent." If there is a suggestion of a distinction in the latter passage, it is no more than this, that, in conformity with

8. Montefiore (1964: 152) states that priests serve in the outer court, which is therefore irrelevant in heaven since Christ is a high priest, not just a priest.

9. Among those who hold this position are Hagner 1983: 116; Hofius 1972: 65–67; Jewett 1981: 150; Lenski 1937: 290–91; Loader 1981: 166–67; Montefiore 1964: 152–53; Riggenbach 1913: 256–57; Thompson 1982: 104–5.

the imagery of the wilderness tabernacle, Christ is envisaged as entering the true tent (of heaven) which contains the true sanctuary (of God's presence). But as the curtain which divided the tent into two chambers has been abolished, it is easy to see how in the true order of things tent and sanctuary can be treated as synonymous terms.

Why would the author of Hebrews have added the first phrase *through his entry into the greater and more perfect tent,* if it meant the same thing as "he entered into the holy of holies"? If this is what the author meant to say, he should have omitted the first phrase as it only adds confusion.[10]

The great virtue with this last view is that it is theologically in harmony with the epistle. There can be no first tent in heaven, since that stands for the old covenant where there was still no direct access to the presence of God. The second position, which implies a barrier is therefore completely inappropriate. Yet while in harmony with the theology of the author, the direct-access position runs into difficulty in explaining why the phrase *through his entry into the greater and more perfect tent* was necessary. If in fact they refer to the same thing and mean the same, why is it necessary to repeat it? In other words, why was the first phrase inserted by the author when it serves no purpose at all?

The interpretations of this passage have poor support and are inappropriate to the context or to the theology of the book. The first view with its many versions has the least to recommend it. Though it has some plausibility, the supporting evidence for it is weak. The second view undercuts a major theological point of the book and thus is hardly acceptable. The third view is in harmony with the theology of the book but runs into the problem of redundancy and lack of clear meaning because of syntactical relationships. In the light of this dilemma, perhaps a new approach is needed and can be allowed.

10. An interesting attempt to deal with the prepositions in this passage is provided by Thompson (1979: 570), who does not show in detail how he would exegete this passage, but he suggests that the use of διὰ τῆς ... σκηνῆς and εἰς τὰ ἄγια "provides two different images of exaltation, both of which are common to Hebrews. On the one hand, it is an entry *through* the heavenly world, as the author frequently suggests (cf. 4:14; 10:20). On the other hand, it is an entry *into* the heavenly world, as the author suggests in several places (cf. 9:23–24; 6:19–20). Both images are used regularly to describe the transcendence of Christ and to contrast his work to the earthly nature of the institutions of the old covenant" (italics added). The question is why he would use both prepositions in the same sentence to mean the same thing.

This new approach assumes that the phrase *the greater and more perfect tent* refers to the most holy place in heaven. This interpretation is more suitable than the others when this verse is compared with Heb 8:2 and 9:24. Also, the expression *greater and more perfect tent, not of this creation, nor made with hands* obviously refers to the counterpart of the earthly. If it refers to heaven, then it can only refer to the ἅγια since in Hebrews heaven cannot have a holy place, which is symbolic of lack of access and lack of reconciliation and forgiveness. To speak of such a thing would go against the major theological point of the book. The immediate context also points in this direction. The author has just been discussing the earthly tabernacle, "the first tent which is still standing," in connection with "gifts and sacrifices . . . which cannot perfect the conscience of the worshiper, but deal only with food and drink and various ablutions, regulations for the body imposed until the time of reformation" (9:8–10). In v. 11 he makes a contrast with that earthly tabernacle.[11] Christ is the high priest, and his tabernacle is greater and more perfect. For these reasons it seems appropriate to begin with the assumption that the "greater and more perfect tent" refers to τὰ ἅγια and then proceed to work out the problems that this interpretation poses syntactically, rather than to accept the smoothest syntactical relationship first and then work out the interpretative problems (the other alternative).

Assuming this interpretation, we then look for clues that will help solve the syntactical problem. The problem, as I have mentioned, is that on this interpretation the sentence *he entered the most holy place through the greater and more perfect tent* [*the most holy place*] does not make good sense. Something has obviously happened to deform this sentence. The passage flows smoothly and understandably through the phrase *not of this creation*, but with the next phrase, οὐδὲ δι' αἵματος τράγων καὶ μόσχων, some dissonance occurs. The reason for this dissonance is that the οὐδέ must correspond to a previous negative (this negative phrase is οὐ χειροποιήτου) and possibly corresponds as well to the following negative phrase, which is in apposition to it (οὐ ταύτης τῆς κτίσεως).

However, the οὐδέ phrase is not in parallel relationship with these negative phrases.

Furthermore, according to BAGD (s.v., οὐδέ) οὐδέ joins negative sentences or clauses to others of the same kind. However, the negative

---

11. Thompson (1982: 568–69) points to the μέν . . . δέ construction as evidence of this, as well as to the contrast between sanctuary and sacrifice as seen in 9:1 and 11.

elements are not of the same kind here. The negative οὐδέ is used with
a διά phrase, while the negative it joins is an adjective (χειροποιήτου)
and its apposition a noun (ταύτης τῆς κτίσεως).

In my view οὐδέ is uncalled for and only οὐ was needed, but the
previous negative phrase led to its introduction. It may seem more
proper to connect it with the whole preceding phase beginning with
διά since they are both διά phrases, but if οὐδέ only joins negative
sentences or clauses, this is not possible since that clause is not
negative.[12] These negatives attracted the negative phrase of v. 12
and thus led to the incomplete thought in v. 11.

This turn in the sentence beginning with οὐδέ has led to a complete change of thought which now fits in with the concluding predicate, but this predicate does not fit the first part of the sentence.

It would appear, then, that the author had another concluding
thought in mind for this first part that would contrast the high
priesthood of Christ and the heavenly sanctuary with those of the
earthly. As the earthly priests in v. 6 entered the first tent τὰς λατρείας ἐπιτελοῦντες, so now Christ ἐπιτελεῖ τὰς λατρείας through the
greater and more perfect tent. This was the thought, it seems, that
the author wished to express first. In contrast to vv. 7–10, he would
show that Christ entered τὰ ἅγια not with δῶρά τε καὶ θυσίαι (τὸ αἷμα
τράγων καὶ μόσχων) which cannot perfect the conscience of the worshiper, but with his own blood. Perhaps after κτίσεως, the author
had intended to add ἐπιτελεῖ τὰς λατρείας. He would show first that
the priesthood of Christ is more effective, and the heavenly sanctuary in which he ministers is greater and more perfect. Then he
would show in contrast to the sacrifices of the old that προσφέρει
θυσίαν ἐφάπαξ δυναμένην κατὰ συνείδησιν τελειῶσαι τὸν λατρεύοντα (cf.
v. 9), and thus he would emphasize that οὐ δι᾽ αἵματος τράγων καὶ
μόσχων διὰ δὲ τοῦ ἰδίον αἵματος εἰσῆλθεν ἐφάπαξ εἰς τὰ ἅγια αἰωνίαν
λύτρωσιν εὑράμενος. What I am proposing, then, is that we supply a
different verb to the first part of this sentence as the original intention of the author and begin a new sentence with οὐδέ changed to
οὐ. Οὐδέ should connect with a previous negative, but to do so here
would make no sense. This emendation would then be in harmony
with the immediate context, and the interpretation of "the greater
and more perfect tent" would harmonize with the predominant
theological motif of the book. Thus the sentence would read Χρισ-

12. Peterson (1982: 142) also points to the fact that "the words 'and not by
means of the blood of goats and calves, but by means of his own blood' introduce a
new element into the structure of the verse instead of offering a further explanation
of the expression 'through the greater and more perfect tent.'"

τὸς δὲ παραγενόμενος ἀρχιερεὺς τῶν γενομένων ἀγαθῶν διὰ τῆς μείζονος καὶ τελειοτέρας σκηνῆς οὐ χειροποιήτου, τοῦτ' ἔστιν οὐ ταύτης τῆς κτίσεως, ἐπιτελεῖ τὰς λατρείας: 'But when Christ appeared as a high priest of the good things that have come, through the greater and more perfect tent he performs his religious service.' The preposition διά then must be understood instrumentally.

Similar thinking also lies behind the NEB translation of this passage: "But now Christ has come, high priest of good things already in being. The tent of his priesthood is a greater and more perfect one, not made by men's hands, that is, not belonging to this created world; the blood of his sacrifice is his own blood, not the blood of goats and calves; and thus he has entered the sanctuary once and for all and secured an eternal deliverance."

The options are to accept syntactical consonance with theological and contextual dissonance, or else theological and contextual consonance with syntactical dissonance. I have opted for the latter and have sought to show how syntactical dissonance arose.

References

Andriessen, Paul
1971   "Das grössere und vollkommenere Zelt (Hebr 9, 11)." *Biblische Zeitschrift* 15:76–91.
Attridge, Harold W.
1986   "The Uses of Antithesis in Hebrews 8–10." *Harvard Theological Review* 79 (Krister Stendahl Fest.): 1–9.
BAGD   *A Greek-English Lexicon of the New Testament and Other Early Christian Literature*, by Walter Bauer. Translated by William F. Arndt and F. Wilbur Gingrich. 2d edition. Revised by F. Wilbur Gingrich and Frederick W. Danker. Chicago: University of Chicago Press, 1979.
Delitzsch, Franz
1871   *Commentary on the Epistle to the Hebrews*. 2 vols. Translated by Thomas L. Kingsbury. Edinburgh: T. & T. Clark.
Dods, Marcus
1956   "The Epistle to the Hebrews." Vol. 4: pp. 219–381 in *Expositor's Greek Testament*. Edited by W. Robertson Nicoll. Reprinted Grand Rapids: Eerdmans.
Galling, Kurt
1950–51 "Durch die Himmel hindurchgeschritten (Heb 4, 14)." *Zeitschrift für die Neutestamentliche Wissenschaft* 43:263–64.
Hagner, Donald A.
1983   *Hebrews*. Good News Commentary. San Francisco: Harper & Row.

Héring, Jean
1970   *The Epistle to the Hebrews.* Translated by A. W. Heathcote and P. J.
        Allcock. London: Epworth.
Hofius, Otfried
1972   *Der Vorhang vor dem Thron Gottes: Eine exegetisch-religionsgeschicht-
        liche Untersuchung zu Hebräer 6, 19f. und 10, 19f.* Wissenschaft-
        liche Untersuchungen zum Neuen Testament 14. Tübingen:
        Mohr (Siebeck).
Hughes, Philip E.
1977   *A Commentary on the Epistle to the Hebrews.* Grand Rapids: Eerdmans.
Jewett, Robert
1981   *Letter to Pilgrims: A Commentary on the Epistle to the Hebrews.* New
        York: Pilgrim.
Koester, Helmut
1962   "'Outside the Camp': Hebrews 13.9–14." *Harvard Theological Re-
        view* 55:299–315.
Laub, Franz
1980   *Bekenntnis und Auslegung: Die paränetische Funktion der Christologie im
        Hebräerbrief.* Biblische Untersuchungen 15. Regensburg: Pustet.
Lenski, Richard C. H.
1937   *The Interpretation of the Epistle to the Hebrews and the Epistle of James.*
        Columbus, Ohio: Wartburg.
Loader, William R. G.
1981   *Sohn und Hoherpriester: Eine traditionsgeschichtliche Untersuchung
        zur Christologie des Hebräerbriefes.* Wissenschaftliche Monogra-
        phien zum Alten und Neuen Testament 53. Neukirchen-Vluyn:
        Neukirchener Verlag.
Michaelis, Wilhelm
1971   "σκηνή." Vol. 7: pp. 368–94 in *Theological Dictionary of the New
        Testament.* Edited by Gerhard Kittel and Gerhard Friedrich.
        Grand Rapids: Eerdmans.
Michel, Otto
1966   *Der Brief an die Hebräer.* 6th edition. Kritisch-exegetischer Kom-
        mentar über das Neue Testament 13. Göttingen: Vanderhoeck
        & Ruprecht.
Moffatt, James
1924   *A Critical and Exegetical Commentary on the Epistle to the Hebrews.*
        International Critical Commentary. Edinburgh: T. & T. Clark.
Montefiore, Hugh
1964   *A Commentary on the Epistle to the Hebrews.* Harper's New Testa-
        ment Commentaries. New York: Harper & Row.
Nissilä, Keijo
1979   *Das Hohepriestermotiv im Hebräerbrief: Eine exegetische Untersuchung.*
        Schriften der finnischen exegetischen Gesellschaft 33. Helsinki:
        Kirjapaino.

Peterson, David
1982   *Hebrews and Perfection: An Examination of the Concept of Perfection in the "Epistle to the Hebrews."* Society for New Testament Studies Monograph Series 47. Cambridge: Cambridge University Press.
Riggenbach, Eduard
1913   *Der Brief an die Hebräer.* Kommentar zum Neuen Testament 14. Leipzig: Deichert.
Schierse, Franz J.
1955   *Verheissung und Heilsvollendung: Zur theologischen Grundfrage des Hebräerbriefes.* Münchener theologische Studien 1/9. Munich: Zink.
Schierse, Franz J., and Otto Knoch
1969   *The Epistle to the Hebrews and the Epistle of St. James.* Translated by Benen Fahy. New York: Herder & Herder.
Spicq, Ceslaus
1952–53   *L'Épître aux Hébreux.* 2 vols. Étude Bibliques. Paris: Gabalda.
Swetnam, James
1966   "On the Imagery and Significance of Hebrews 9, 9–10." *Catholic Biblical Quarterly* 28:155–73.
Thompson, James W.
1979   "Hebrews 9 and Hellenistic Concepts of Sacrifice." *Journal of Biblical Literature* 98:567–78.
1982   *The Beginnings of Christian Philosophy: The Epistle to the Hebrews.* Catholic Biblical Quarterly Monograph Series 13. Washington, D.C.: Catholic Biblical Association of America.
Vanhoye, Albert
1965   "'Par la tente plus grande et plus parfaite . . . ' (He 9, 11)." *Biblica* 46:1–28.
Weiss, Bernhard
1888   *Kritisch-exegetisches Handbuch über den Brief an die Hebräer.* Kritisch-exegetischer Kommentar über das Neue Testament 13. Göttingen: Vandenhoeck & Ruprecht.
Westcott, Brooke F.
1955   *The Epistle to the Hebrews.* Reprinted Grand Rapids: Eerdmans.
Wickham, E. C.
1910   *The Epistle to the Hebrews.* Westminster Commentaries. London: Methuen.
Williamson, R.
1974–75   "The Eucharist and the Epistle to the Hebrews." *New Testament Studies* 21:300–310.
Young, Norman H.
1980–81   "The Gospel according to Hebrews 9." *New Testament Studies* 27:198–210.

The New Revised
Standard Version

Bruce M. Metzger
Princeton Theological Seminary

It is a pleasure to contribute to the Festschrift that honors a friend and colleague, J. Harold Greenlee. During several of the ten years that an international committee was working together in editing *The Greek New Testament*, issued by the American Bible Society in 1966, Dr. Greenlee gave the committee invaluable assistance before, during, and after our annual meetings. It was he who was largely responsible for drawing up for that edition the apparatus giving information as to varying possibilities in punctuation. Knowing his interest and competence in all aspects of Bible translating, I would like to offer some comments regarding the New Revised Standard Version, released on September 30, 1990.

Beginning in 1973 to update the RSV, the thirty members of the Standard Bible Committee finished their work in 1988, at which time two smaller editorial committees, composed of myself with two members of the OT section and two members of the NT section, tried to bring about a still-greater degree of homogeneity in the rendering.

As would be expected, the basic Greek text of the NT was UBS[3]. I was able also to make available information concerning changes that are to be introduced into the critical apparatus of the forthcoming

111

4th edition of the UBS Greek Testament. In some cases a marginal rendering was included in the NRSV where UBS⁴ will supply a set of variant readings (no changes are to be made in the text itself of the 4th edition). Only in very rare instances did we reject the text of the UBS³ by adopting an alternative reading that seemed to be superior.

First, with regard to punctuation, we made use of the double square brackets that are employed in the Greek text in order to enclose a few passages that are generally regarded to be later additions to the text, but which we retained because of their evident antiquity and importance in the textual tradition. We did not feel ourselves bound to the changes introduced in the punctuation of UBS³, particularly with reference to the usage of commas. In fact, for UBS³ the Institute for New Testament Text Research at Münster replaced the original style of punctuating the Greek text (which had been essentially that of the Westcott and Hort edition of 1881) with a different system of punctuating Greek that might be called the Teutonic or Continental system—a change that I know was a painful shock to Dr. Greenlee.

As was mentioned above, we stayed close to the wording of UBS³, but felt (or at least a majority of the members of the NT section felt) that in several passages the preferred reading was to be found in the critical apparatus. For example, in Acts 26:28, besides construing the sentence as a question, a majority of the NRSV committee preferred to adopt the variant reading γενέσθαι, and to render Festus's words to Paul, "Are you so quickly persuading me to become a Christian?" A footnote tells the reader that the sentence can also be read as a statement, using the word ποιῆσαι with its rare meaning of "play": "Quickly you will persuade me to play the Christian."

Another instance where we departed from UBS³ is 1 Thess 2:7, with its notoriously perplexing variants νήπιοι/ἤπιοι. Here we render the sentence, "But we were gentle among you, like a nurse tenderly caring for her own children." A footnote informs the reader that instead of the word *gentle,* "Other ancient authorities read *infants.*"

Another instance where we depart from UBS³ is the last verse of the NT (Rev 22:21) where the NRSV reads, "The grace of the Lord Jesus be with all the saints. Amen," whereas the Greek text in the UBS³ has neither "the saints" nor "Amen." The footnote in the NRSV tells the reader, "Other ancient authorities lack *all*; others lack *the saints*; others lack *Amen.*"

As regards paragraphing, at 1 Tim 3:1 we range πιστὸς ὁ λόγος with what follows, not with what precedes, as in UBS³.

Among new words that are not in the RSV *Wortschatz,* the NRSV contains the following:

NRSV	RSV	Reference
attorney	spokesman	Acts 24:1
bungler	sinner	Eccl 9:18
chiseled	carved	2 Cor 3:7
disciplinarian	custodian	Gal 3:24–25
encroach	draw near	Deut 2:37
exploited	grasped	Phil 2:6
fiancée	betrothed	1 Cor 7:36–38
lazybones	sluggard	Prov 6:6, 9
liberator	judge	Acts 7:35
litigation	judgment	Hos 10:4
loungers	those who stretch themselves	Amos 6:7
mauled	tore	2 Kgs 2:24
nagged	pressed hard	Judg 14:17, 16:16
pestered	urged	Judg 16:16
rogues	unjust	Luke 18:11
ruffians	wicked fellows of the rabble	Acts 17:5
scoundrels	base fellows	Deut 13:13
spellbound	astonished	Mark 11:18
thug	a man who destroys	Prov 28:24
wadi	valley	Deut 2:27, etc.

A new proper name is provided in a footnote to the rendering "loyal companion" at Phil 4:3, namely "Or *loyal Syzygus*."

Material equivalent to three or four verses is added at the end of 1 Samuel 10 on the testimony of a newly edited Qumran manuscript, supported in part by Josephus, *Antiquities* 6:68–71 (6:5:1). Verse 27 continues:

> Now Nahash, king of the Ammonites, had been grievously oppressing the Gadites and the Reubenites. He would gouge out the right eye of each of them and would not grant Israel a deliverer. No one was left of the Israelites across the Jordan whose right eye Nahash, king of the Ammonites, had not gouged out. But there were seven thousand men who had escaped from the Ammonites and had entered Jabesh-gilead.

On the other hand, the following words that are present in the RSV were not kept in the NRSV: ass (except "wild ass"), dumb, fetch, girdle, hart, lest, scourge (verb), victuals. The two words *for ever* are now written as one word, and *none*, when referring to a person, is written *no one*. Instead of the rather haphazard use of *which* and *that* in the RSV, we have restricted the use of *which* to instances where it follows a comma, a preposition, or the word *that*.

Among phrases that could be regarded as typical of biblical English, the following among many that could be mentioned have been altered in the NRSV:

burn incense	changed to	offer incense
David the king	"	King David
fine flour	"	choice flour
Jeremiah the prophet	"	the prophet Jeremiah
peace offering	"	offering of well-being

As regards masculine-oriented language the following comments may be of interest. The committee made no changes with respect to language pertaining to the Deity. As every biblical scholar knows, in both Hebrew and Greek texts masculine pronouns are used when referring to God. Twenty-six books of the NT refer to God as Father. None of this was altered. But, as is also well known, the English language has an inherent bias toward the masculine gender, a bias that in the case of the Bible has often restricted or obscured the meaning of the original text. The mandates that the RSV Committee received from the National Council of Churches specified, among other things, that masculine-oriented language should be eliminated as far as this can be done without altering passages that reflect the historical situation of ancient patriarchal culture. In order to fulfill such a mandate, the committee tried to steer a middle course between using, on the one hand, contrived English (such as he/she and the like) and, on the other, incorrect grammar (such as "their" in referring to a singular subject). The following are specimens of the various kinds of solutions that were employed.

Gen 1:27   So God created humankind in his image, in the image of God he created them; male and female he created them.
Here a footnote on "humankind" reads "Heb *adam*" (note the lowercase *a*), and another footnote on the first "them" reads "Heb *him*."

Deut 8:3   One does not live by bread alone, but by every word that comes from the mouth of the LORD.

Judg 21:25   All the people did what was right in their own eyes

Ps 1:1   Happy are those who do not follow the advice of the wicked.

Mic 6:8   He has told you, O mortal, what is good.

Matt 7:9   Is there anyone among you who, if your child asks for bread, will give a stone?

Mark 2:27   The sabbath was made for humankind, not humankind for the sabbath.

John 3:36   Whoever believes in the Son has eternal life; whoever disobeys the Son will not see life, but must endure God's wrath.

John 12:32   And I, when I am lifted up from the earth, will draw all people to myself.

Eph 3:16   That you may be strengthened in your inner being with power through his Spirit.

James 1:14   One is tempted by one's own desire, being lured and enticed by it.

Rev 21:3   See, the home of God is among mortals.

Usually when ἀδελφοί occurs in the Pauline letters the rendering is "brothers and sisters," with a footnote "Gk *brothers*." When ἀδελφοί occurs repeatedly in the same passage (as in 1 Thessalonians 4–5), some variation is provided by using "beloved" or a similar word, with a footnote "Gk *brothers*."

No translation of the Scriptures is perfect, as everyone who has ever tried to make one is ready to acknowledge. Luther, it is said, issued nineteen revisions of his German Bible. At the close of more than fifteen years of work on the NRSV, probably all members of the committee felt a mixture of relief and regret—relief that the work was finished, but also regret that still further "fine tuning" would have made a better rendering. In any case, there comes a time when one must say enough is enough.

Translating New Testament Poetry

David Alan Black

Talbot School of Theology

Introduction

A great concern in the process of Bible translation, and a task to which the honoree of this Festschrift has devoted considerable attention, is the loss of connotative impact, especially in highly literary texts, even though the essential denotative content may be communicated. In rendering poetic language the task of Bible translators is a particularly difficult one. They recognize the need to convey the essential denotative content of the text, but they are also concerned with the inevitable loss of connotative impact. They know that rhetorical features are just as important as lexical or syntactical features in contributing to meaningfulness, yet they desire not to sacrifice content to style.

Here one runs head-on into questions of translation *equivalence* (how accurate is my translation?) and translation *acceptability* (how much variation will be tolerated?). One also encounters the stubborn fact that the meaning of any utterance is not a single phenomenon, but a synthesis of various elements—phonetic, phonological, morphological, syntactic, lexical, and semantic. The importance of each element varies from one situation or language user to another. In "Some Current Trends in Translation Theory," David Crystal (1976: 325) has taken up this perplexing issue:

> Total linguistic equivalence—in the sense of preserving equivalence at all levels—is . . . an impossibility. Lexical and semantic factors are usually permitted to outrank the others, but in certain contexts (usually literary or aesthetic) the other factors are regularly considered as having an important bearing on the finished work. The notion of levels has therefore more than merely theoretical importance.

To illustrate the complexities of the issue raised by Crystal, attention may be drawn to G. Mounin's observation that the parallelism of μεγαλύνει-μεγάλα in the Lukan Magnificat (Luke 1:46, 49) is not rendered in any French translation. Mounin (1979: 339) argues that "all our modern translations, aiming at dynamic equivalence (communicating the meaning of the text in today's language), are all unconsciously governed by a Greco-Latin rhetoric (which for example recommends writers to avoid repetition of the same word in the same passage)." Mounin's point is well taken. In most modern translations the *contents* of the NT are easily accessible. But the NT's formal poetry, as distinct from what it says, is not. Translators tend (subconsciously, perhaps) to be indifferent to the NT's forms and formulatory patterns, and rarely do these forms and patterns govern the way the translator renders the text into English. Consequently, while we have a fairly good picture of *what* the NT says, we have only a vague notion, if any, of *how* the NT says what it says. In justification for lodging this grievance I need only point out that if we do not know *how* a document expresses its ideas, we do not fully grasp *what* it wishes to say. Mounin (1979: 340) is sensitive to this issue when he writes: "The most realistic conclusion is doubtless that we must more and more include, within our dynamic equivalence translations, respect for certain elements of formal equivalence, when prior analysis of the text has shown that these formal structures have a function." This is more easily said than done, however.

The point that emerges thus far is well summarized in the words of Crystal (1976: 327): "There are many legitimate translations of a particular text, depending on the emphasis the individual translator (or team) places on the separate variables. Instead of talking about the need for *an* acceptable translation, accordingly, one needs to think in terms of *kinds* of acceptable translations." Hence the thoughtful translator has to face the question of which of the various elements of meaning contributes most to the whole of the text. Mounin's complaint above was directed precisely toward the tendency to ignore connotative elements of meaningfulness in translating the Bible. Generally speaking, the meaning of the original text is expressed in certain clearly defined structures and patterns, yet little, if any, attempt is made to carry over into English the grammatical structures and rhetorical patterns of the original language.

Toward a Poetics of the New Testament

Despite the somewhat disconcerting sketch given above, over the past twenty years there has been remarkable development in the area of research into the poetry of the NT. As is well known, one of the qualities that chiefly distinguishes great literature from nonliterary writing is the close relationship—indeed the actual fusion—of form and idea. We may sometimes pretend to detach the meaning from the form of a work, but we soon realize that this extracted "meaning" is far less than the total meaning. To be sure, nonliterary writing has significant form, for its diction, figures, and rhythms are all part of the meaning of the work. But in poetry the union of form and content is so intimate that it is almost impossible to extract meaning without paying considerable attention to form. The text is not only trying to get information across; it is making an appeal to its readers. As Eugene Nida (1975: 18) notes, "emotive meanings are not related primarily to language as structure, but rather to the manner in which this structure manifests itself, especially in the actual discourse." In other words, translation involves not only analyzing what a person says, but also how that person says it. Thus P. C. Stine (1972: 202) argues that we "should . . . make a real effort to employ a variety of styles as the text might suggest them." Nida (1982b: 332) agrees: "Truly poetic passages should be translated as poetry, and if so, the format should reflect the way in which poetry in the receptor language is normally printed." What these translators are emphasizing is the power of poetry to produce in the mind an effect very nearly the same as that created by the stimulation of the sensory organs. For example, in the following stanza from "The Rime of the Ancient Mariner," note the intertwining of several alliterative sequences involving *f, b, w,* and *s*:

> The fair breeze blew, the white foam flew,
> The furrow followed free;
> We were the first that ever burst
> Into that silent sea.

This heavy use of alliteration imparts great intensity to the lines, in keeping with the drama of briskly sailing at sea. In such a situation the reader becomes an active participant in creating the emotion of the poem.

This illustration brings me to the most important phase in the discussion of poetic form. An understanding of such poetic devices as alliteration, rhyme, and stanza structure is only preliminary to a realization of the total effect of poetic form. From time to time NT expositors have suggested that one device or another may have a given effect; actually, the effect of any strategem may be judged only in its total setting, and there the result may be wholly different from its usual effect. In other words, the practice of judging the effects of poetic language is based on a solid knowledge of the techniques employed by the author, but it also proceeds by the application of this knowledge through sensitivity and imagination.

For example, the author of Hebrews is now generally acknowledged to be one of the great masters of poetic techniques. In the opening paragraph of Hebrews, a passage famous for its literary form, the author has managed the ingenious integration of poetic technique and meaning. Heb 1:1–4 achieves its artistic beauty by the skillful coordination of clauses (periodism), compactness (ellipsis), contrast, the presence of hymnic language (1:3), significant figures of speech (metonymy and metaphor), repetition, and rhythm, to name only the more obvious devices (Black 1987). We might call special attention to the meter of certain lines to see how the distribution of stresses contributes to the effects generated by such rhythm:

ὧν ἀπαύγασμα τῆς δόξης καὶ χαρακτὴρ τῆς ὑποστάσεως αὐτοῦ
φέρων τε τὰ πάντα τῷ ῥήματι τῆς δυνάμεως αὐτοῦ

These lines terminate identically in anapest and spondee, so that the text can be fully appreciated, if at all, only by observing the intensity of stresses and the greater than usual attention to rhythm. If we look now at alliteration, we find a good many π sounds in the opening line:

Πολυμερῶς καὶ πολυτρόπως πάλαι ὁ θεὸς λαλήσας τοῖς
πατράσιν ἐν τοῖς προφήταις

Note that the device of alliteration is associated with the denotations and connotations of the words employed by the author—"In many times . . . in many ways . . . formerly . . . fathers . . . prophets." The words of the surrounding sounds not included in the alliterating sequence seem to carry less import than those alliterated.

Three conclusions are in order here. First, a small difference in sound quality may be very important. Second, I reiterate that one's perception of the emotional qualities of sounds is conditioned by the meanings of the words that carry the sounds. Finally, however, the most important point is this: the analysis of poetic form is not an end in itself. There is little value in determining that a stanza has a pair of rhythmic clausulae, or that a passage has used alliteration of certain sounds, or that it has employed this or that figure of speech, if one does not go on to collect these separate observations into some kind of comprehensive account of the text's meaning. To do that one must be sensitive to certain aspects of the contents of poetry.

This brings us to the important point that the literal meaning a poem may convey and the poem itself are separate things, operating at different levels of meaning. One may say, "I am falling asleep," and expect to be understood. But in Tennyson's lines, "To Sleep I give my powers away; / My will is bondsman to the dark," the fact of sleep is not as important as the feelings associated with it. Tennyson treats the subject not as information but as felt experience—the feeling of helplessness and subjection to something beyond one's control. Stated in prose, the main idea of Tennyson's lines is simple. The poem, however, says much more than this, for Tennyson skillfully opens an area of unstated possibilities by quietly attaching feelings to the inevitability of sleep.

This way of distinguishing between poetry and prose naturally requires many qualifications. For one thing, poetry is not purely emotional, but requires many talents of the intellect both to compose it and to read it (e.g., the ability to think logically, the capacity to make subtle connections, etc.). It is thus safe to say that poetry offers more of a challenge to interpretation than does prose. Also, while poetry can generally be distinguished from prose by its emotional and imaginative qualities, it is more easily recognized by its secondary characteristics such as similes and metaphors, which are particularly well suited to expressing emotion. Because poetry is marked by one or more of these characteristics, it can go a long way toward exchanging functions with prose without ever losing its identity as poetry. Hence poetry may be factual and still be poetry. The Latin poet Horace once said that poetry has the function of teaching as well as delighting. Indeed, once one turns to the poetry of the NT, one is likely to find that most of it has a moral quality. It seeks, not merely to express a view of something, but to suggest the kind of behavior appropriate to that view. There is a large body of religious verse in the Pauline writings whose dominant purpose is moral teaching. Everything else these poems contain is merely a way of supplementing some moral lesson. The *Carmen Christi* of Phil 2:6–11 is one of the best-known illustrations of such poetry. The poem reminds us that everyday activities are to be controlled by the mind of Christ and not by personal ambition, thus illustrating Paul's ethical injunction in 2:1–4 (see Black 1985, 1988).

But poetry is also capable of generating extended and systematic bodies of knowledge. Because it uses the power of the imagination to probe experience, it enables us to formulate firm bases of belief for our actions and principles, and acts as a creative force in the world of ideas. The "faithful saying" in 2 Tim 2:11 is an excellent example of poetry working in this way (my translation):

> In dying with Christ true life we gain,
> Enduring, we with him shall reign;
> Who him deny he will disclaim,
> Our faith may fail, his cannot wane—
> FOR THUS HE IS, HE CANNOT CHANGE!

This poem does its work by using a set of antitheses, vigorously imagined and sharply sketched, to offer the reader a new and authentic reality. The unanswered questions that arise within the poem are a part of its mystifying effect. It presents itself for contemplation, without explaining anything. Whatever *meaning*, in the narrow sense of the term, it may have is not within the poem itself, but is only made possible by it.

Poetry such as this often uses an imagined *dramatic situation*. This situation, overt or implied, may be the matter of chief interest in the poem, or it may be the means of conveying an attitude or proposition. The dramatic situation in 2 Tim 2:11 is only implied, as we have seen, but it is of central importance in the poem and all the more impressive because readers must reconstruct it for themselves.

To summarize, I assert that poetry communicates *in many ways at once*. The various levels of meaning interact with each other and may reinforce or counteract each other to produce a net effect that is greater than the impact of the several components taken separately. In short, a work of art must be taken as a whole; it is an inseparable fusion—a complete flowing together—of idea and form. In a broad sense, then, NT poetry is both productive and theoretical, irrational and rational. This contrast, in Aristotelian terms, constitutes the difference between "making" (ποίησις) and "doing" (πρᾶξις), for poetry is essentially a creative art, the end of which is not simply practical action, but also beauty itself.

On Interpretation and Translation

So far I have discussed the fundamental elements of NT poetry from the point of view of its production or as features of the writer producing it. But the analysis is equally valid and important if regarded from the interpreter's point of view. Poetry—to be poetry—must have appeal to the reader's imagination and powers of observation. Herein lies the defense of the so-called reader-response critic, whose work is not primarily an analysis, but a description of the experiences of certain highly developed sensibilities in contact with a work of literature. The chief value of literary criticism is, after all, not in supplying final verdicts, but in affording certain esthetic sensibilities that will equip one with the suppleness of mind for an effective individual analysis. This principle applies even in the field of traditional grammatical-historical exegesis, where critics are exceedingly careful (as they should be) to pay due attention to matters historical and theological. Of course, the study of form and style as factors in biblical exegesis has little more than begun, and is beset by peculiar difficulties; but when the facts are known, biblical scholars will find still another field for the application of the principles of biblical interpretation.

In attempting to analyze the faculty of imagination from the point of view of the observer of poetic devices, an examination of the critical terms employed will serve both to keep a person within the range of this inquiry and to confront readers with some of the most vital problems facing the literary critic of the Bible. I begin by emphasizing that imagination, like all human faculties, may be either active or passive. Effective poetic analysis goes beyond mere passive observation, but allows itself to be led eagerly along by the imagination in perceiving meanings and relations that lie beneath the surface. An activated imagination is what recently caused my five-year-old son, as we were waiting for a traffic light to turn green, to speak of God controlling the traffic signals by means of buttons and wires connecting heaven to earth. The deduction was incorrect, of course; but the story works by illustrating the power of true imaginative vision, in which the result is flashed upon the inward eye, not arrived at by logic or ingenuity.

It follows, therefore, that another basic truth must be admitted: not only is poetry an art of language, but the words the poet uses are characteristically enriched by human associations, affecting words through their involvement with the mundane affairs of humane experience. This process of enrichment explains why poets rarely create new words, but are quite content to draw their vocabulary from the same sources used by everyone else. "Poetry is not a special kind of language," notes Charles Wheeler (1966: 6). "It is, rather, a special way in which language is used." In order to see what qualities poetry possesses, it is thus necessary to see how poetry (and prose) is related to language as a whole. The diagram below is a way of doing this visually, through a schematic picture of the relationships.

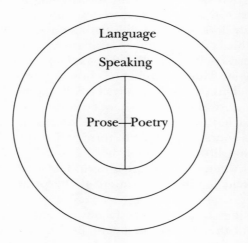

As this diagram reveals, poetry is but the artful use of language, though—as the diagram also indicates—no radical separation between prose and poetry is possible. In the translation of prose, what is more important than verbatim rendering, and what is frequently much more possible to attain, is an accurate reproduction of the author's thoughts. Poetry, however, is like a spoiled child that constantly asserts itself, incessantly shouting, "Look at me! Here I am!" Prose may be stated (and translated) in many different ways; poetry is not an alternative way of saying something, but the only way. In other words, the systems by which messages are encoded and conveyed also influence what can be conveyed in them—not as much as Marshall McLuhan claimed, perhaps, but nevertheless in real and important ways. Poetic texts are therefore produced and interpreted through the mediation of poetic devices as well as through language itself.

Let me try to be more precise, now, in situating poetic interpretation among the other approaches to biblical exegesis. As I alluded to above, today there are advocates of both author-oriented and reader-oriented criticism. E. D. Hirsch (1976), the principal advocate of author-oriented criticism, has argued—in my view persuasively—that one cannot speak of a determinate interpretation unless postulating an authorial intention that governs that interpretation. Hirsch's approach assumes—again, in my view correctly—that the author of a literary text is by definition superior to the reader, and that the burden of the reader is to recover the author's intention. This approach has many obvious strengths. But it is clear that the weaknesses in this approach—and this is where reader-oriented critics are most vocal—lies in the fact that students are not necessarily adequate readers. Sadly, author-oriented criticism often leads to a rigid sort of authoritarianism that stifles the student's creative impulses and makes reading (and interpretation) a chore. Yet surely in the science of biblical interpretation there must be some middle ground between the anarchy of interpretive variation inherent within reader-response criticism and the law-and-order authoritarianism that characterizes author-oriented criticism. To be sure, biblical texts must be understood as the product of a person (or persons), at a given point in human history, in a given form of discourse. The analyst is thus entitled to speculate about this or that grammatical possibility or about this or that historical setting. However, it seems to me that it is relevant for biblical interpretation to emphasize the text *as a text*, within the legitimate limits imposed by historical-grammatical exegesis. Poetic texts work differently than prose texts, as the reader-oriented critics have demonstrated very well, but like prose texts, are dominated by language codes and conventions (as the author-oriented critics are quick to point out).

It is precisely this tendency to approach a poetic text as if it were prose—and thus overlook its essential nature—that worries the literary critic of the Bible. It is probable that all the NT writings contain at least traces of poetry, and the more such poetry is recognized as being present, the more difficult the problem becomes. In order to isolate poetry in the context of a biblical text we need a sensitivity that will enable us to recognize different aspects of poetic language. To employ a well-known analogy, magicians do not expect their audiences actually to see ladies sawed in half. The feature that makes the magician's performance more than simple detection is the audience's knowledge that it is a trick. Likewise, what makes poetry so intriguing is knowing that it is poetry, though of course one's satisfaction depends not merely on one's ability to perceive the presence of poetry but on one's ability to perceive how the "trick" is done. Translators who can do both participate in the text to the fullest extent possible, giving full reign to both their imagination and their analytical intelligence. To them, poetry reveals an amazing amount of information, since behind each poem is an author who put everything into the poem he or she sees, and put it there for a reason. *To penetrate into the life of the poem*: this is as much the translator's privilege as it was that of the original audience.

Conclusion

This essay begins with certain fundamental questions about the nature of NT poetry, to which I have tried to supply answers of a purely introductory fashion. I noted that poetry is a special way of using language, within the context of other uses of language. I also noted the qualities of language that poetry brings into being. The result is an admittedly overly condensed essay that of necessity minimizes the pragmatic dimensions of NT poetry and concentrates instead on the task of developing insight into it. My approach may be characterized as analytical, in the modern tradition of "close reading" or *explication de texte*. But the chronic problem facing all theories of reader-response criticism is that they rarely explain why poetry is there. I have attempted to focus on the question *To what end does one study poetry?* My answer has been to suggest that NT poetry is not just an objective form of language per se, but indeed a special use of language, and that by its very nature NT poetry demands the attention of the translator. It seems to me that the real test of poetry is the test of translation. To "carry over" (trans-late) a poem from one language to another—as impossible as that may seem—is therefore a worthy and noble task for any translator.

We are thus, by this inevitably roundabout way, back to the question with which this essay begins. Being so radically different in the way they use language, it is no wonder that poetry and prose tend to repel each other. If what I have argued is correct, however, one may no longer be content to focus on the extrinsic character of prose to the neglect of the intrinsic character of poetry. One must now think of language in poetry as having something to say *beyond* the denotative meaning of words, however difficult this connotative meaning may be to discern—and translate. But then, with full attention to the texture as well as the import of what one reads, one comes to share in the achievement of the poet, discovering that even texts supposedly familiar appear fresh and new. In the collaborative act between writer and reader the nuances that were otherwise only potential come into full being, and the mere physical form of the Word awakens into the reality of a poem.

Bibliography

Black, David Alan
  1985   "Paul and Christian Unity: A Formal Analysis of Philippians 2:1–4." *Journal of the Evangelical Theological Society* 28:299–308.
  1987   "Hebrews 1:1–4: A Study in Discourse Analysis. *Westminster Theological Journal* 49:175–94.
  1988   "The Authorship of Philippians 2:6–11: Some Literary-Critical Observations." *Criswell Theological Review* 2:269–89.
Crim, K. R.
  1972   "Translating the Poetry of the Bible." *Bible Translator* 23:102–9.
Crystal, David
  1976   "Some Current Trends in Translation Theory." *Bible Translator* 27:322–29.
Culshaw, W.
  1968   "Translating Biblical Poetry." *Bible Translator* 19:1–6.
Hirsch, E. D.
  1976   *The Aims of Interpretation.* Chicago: University of Chicago Press.
Mounin, G.
  1979   "Hebraic Rhetoric and Faithful Translation." *Bible Translator* 30:336–40.
Nida, Eugene A.
  1975   *Exploring Semantic Structures.* Munich: Fink.
  1982a   "Poetry and the Bible Translator." *Bible Translator* 33:435–38.
  1982b   "Quality in Translation." *Bible Translator* 33:329–32.
Stine, P. C.
  1972   "Let's Make Our Translations More Interesting." *Bible Translator* 23:202–6.
Wendland, E. R.
  1981   "Receptor Language Style and Bible Translation." *Bible Translator* 32:319–28.
Wheeler, Charles
  1966   *The Design of Poetry.* New York: Norton.

Scripture Index